D0537840

Registration Exam

TOMORROW'S PHARMACIST

Welcome to the *Tomorrow's Pharmacist* series – helping you with your future career in pharmacy.

Like the journal, book titles under this banner are specifically aimed at pre-registration trainees and pharmacy students, to help them prepare for their future career. These books provide guidance on topics such as the interview and application process for the pre-registration year, the registration examination and future employment in a specific speciality.

The annual journal *Tomorrow's Pharmacist* will contain information and excerpts from the books in this series.

You can find more information on the journal at www.pjonline.com/tp

Titles in the series so far include:
The Pre-registration Interview: Preparation for the application process
Registration Exam Questions

Registration Exam Questions

Nadia Bukhari

BPharm, MRPharmS, PG Dip, PG Cert

Masters of Pharmacy Programme Manager
and Pre-registration Coordinator
School of Pharmacy, University of London, UK

London • Chicago Pharmaceutical Press

Published by the Pharmaceutical Press

1 Lambeth High Street, London SE1 7JN, UK
University City Center, Suite 5E, 3624 Market Street, Philadelphia, PA
19104, USA

(**PP**) is a trade mark of Pharmaceutical Press

Pharmaceutical Press is the publishing division of the Royal
Pharmaceutical Society

First published 2008
Reprinted 2009, 2010, 2012

Typeset by Photoprint Typesetters, Torquay, Devon
Printed in Great Britain by TJ International, Padstow, Cornwall

ISBN 978 0 85369 699 5

A catalogue record for this book is available from the British Library.

MIX
Paper from
responsible sources
FSC   FSC® C013056
www.fsc.org

1006987875

Disclaimer

The views expressed in this book are solely those of the author and do not
necessarily reflect the views or policies of the Royal Pharmaceutical Society
of Great Britain. This book does NOT guarantee success in the registration
exam but can be used as an aid for revision.

I would like to dedicate this book to my son, Hamza Bukhari who is the light of my life.

Contents

Preface

After completing four years of study and graduating with a Master of Pharmacy (MPharm) degree, graduates are required to undertake training as a preregistration pharmacist before they can sit the registration examination.

Preregistration training is the period of employment that a graduate must embark on and effectively complete before they can register as a pharmacist in Great Britain. In most cases it is a one-year period following the pharmacy degree; for sandwich course students it is integrated within the undergraduate programme.

On successful passing of the registration examination, pharmacy graduates can register as a pharmacist in Great Britain.

The registration examination harmonizes the testing of skills in practice during the preregistration year. It tests:

- knowledge
- the application of knowledge
- calculation
- time management
- managing stress
- comprehension
- recall
- interpretation
- evaluation.

There are two examination papers: an open book and a closed book paper. Questions are based on practice-based situations and are designed to test the thinking and knowledge that lie behind any action.

EXAMINATION FORMAT

The registration examination consists of two papers:

- closed book (no reference material can be used)
  90 questions in 90 minutes (1.5 hours)

- open book (three specified reference sources permitted)
  80 questions in 150 minutes (2.5 hours)
- 60 non-calculation-style (recommended time for these 1.5 hours)
- 20 calculation-style (recommended time 1 hour)

The calculation-style questions are grouped together as a section of the paper.

The reference sources that the Royal Pharmaceutical Society of Great Britain permit for the registration examination are:

- *British National Formulary*
- *Drug Tariff for England and Wales* or *Drug Tariff for Scotland*
- *Medicines, Ethics and Practice Guide*

The registration examination is crucial for pharmacy graduates wishing to register in Great Britain.

Preparation is the key. This book is a bank of just under 400 questions, which are similar to the style of the registration examination. The questions are based on law and ethics, and clinical pharmacy and therapeutic aspects of the registration examination syllabus.

The Pharmaceutical Press have published books on calculations and responding to symptoms; thus these types of questions have not been included in the book.

This book cannot guarantee that you pass the registration examination; however, it can help you to practise the clinical pharmacy and law and ethics type questions, both very important aspects of the registration examination — and, as they say, 'practice makes perfect'.

Good luck with the examination.

Nadia Bukhari
December 2007

Acknowledgements

The author wishes to acknowledge the support received from students and colleagues at the School of Pharmacy, University of London.

I especially thank my parents and my mother-in-law for their continuous support and encouragement.

I thank all my friends, especially Saima Khan, Asma Lahar and Sara Latif for being there whenever I needed them.

I would like to express thanks to my editors at the Pharmaceutical Press, who have been very supportive, and especially to the senior commissioning editor, Christina De Bono, for her guidance.

I wish to express gratitude to Shoaib Taimur, who was an excellent typist and helped me out in my time of need.

I wish to thank my husband, Murtaza Bukhari, deeply, for providing all the support I needed to make this book happen — you are the best!

About the author

After qualifying, Nadia Bukhari worked as a pharmacy manager at Westbury Chemist, Streatham, London, for a year, after which she moved on to work for St Bartholomew's Hospital and the London NHS trust as a clinical pharmacist in surgery. It was at this time that Nadia developed an interest in teaching, as part of her role as a teacher practitioner for the School of Pharmacy, University of London.

Two and a half years later, she began work for the School of Pharmacy, University of London, as the preregistration tutor for the school and the academic facilitator. This position involved teaching therapeutics to Masters of Pharmacy students and assisting the director of undergraduate studies.

Recently Nadia has taken on the role of the MPharm programme manager for the undergraduate degree.

Nadia was a question writer for the registration exam for the RPSGB for 4 years, hence the interest to write the book.

How to use this book

The book is divided into two main sections: Open book and Closed book.

Each section has four different styles of multiple choice questions, which are also used in the registration examination: simple completion, multiple completion, classification and statements.

SIMPLE COMPLETION QUESTIONS

Each of the questions or statements in this section is followed by five suggested answers. Select the best answer in each situation.

For example:

A patient on your ward has been admitted with a gastric ulcer, which is currently being treated. She has a history of arthritis and cardiac problems. Which of her drugs is most likely to have caused the gastric ulcer?

A   paracetamol
B   naproxen
C   furosemide
D   propranolol
E   codeine phosphate

MULTIPLE COMPLETION QUESTIONS

Each one of the questions or incomplete statements in this section is followed by three responses. For each question, ONE or MORE of the responses is/are correct. Decide which of the responses is/are correct, then choose:

A if 1, 2, and 3 are correct

B if **1** and **2** only are correct
C if **2** and **3** only are correct
D if **1** only is correct
E if **3** only is correct

For example:
A patient presents a FP10D to you.
Which of the below CANNOT be prescribed on this type of form?

1   ciprofloxacin
2   diclofenac   c
3   paracetamol

CLASSIFICATION

In this section, for each numbered question, select the one lettered option that most closely corresponds to the answer. Within each group of questions each lettered option may be used once, more than once, or not at all.

For example:
Which of the following vitamins:

1   can cause ocular defects in deficiency states? A
2   is necessary for the production of blood-clotting factors? E
3   prevents scurvy? B
4   can be used for the treatment of rickets? C

    A   vitamin A
    B   vitamin C
    C   vitamin D
    D   vitamin E
    E   vitamin K

STATEMENT

The questions in this section consist of a statement in the top row followed by a second statement beneath.

You need to:
decide whether the **first** statement is true or false.
decide whether the **second** statement is true or false.
Then choose:
A if both statements are true and the second statement is **a correct explanation** of the first statement
B if both statements are true but the second statement is **NOT a correct explanation** of the first statement
C if the first statement is true but the second statement is false
D if the first statement is false but the second statement is true
E if both statements are false

For example:

First statement
Microgynon is an example of a combined oral contraceptive pill

Second statement
Combined pills contain oestrogen and testosterone

The closed book questions should be attempted without using any references sources, as you would for the examination.

The open book questions should be attempted with the Society's permitted reference sources for the registration examination which are:

• *British National Formulary*
• *Drug Tariff for England and Wales* or *Drug Tariff for Scotland*
• *Medicines, Ethics and Practice Guide*

Answers to the questions are at the end of the open book and closed book sections. Brief explanations or a suitable reference for sourcing the answer are given, to aid understanding and to facilitate learning.

Important: This text refers to the current edition of the BNF when the text was written. Please always consult the LATEST version for the most up-to-date information.

Open book questions

SIMPLE COMPLETION QUESTIONS

Each of the questions or statements in this section is followed by five suggested answers. Select the best answer in each situation.

1 Mrs Felicity is one of your regular patients who has acute porphyria. The GP is aware that there may be some drugs which may be unsafe to prescribe for her.
From the following list, which drug is safe to prescribe for Mrs Felicity?

    A   methyldopa
    B   oxybutynin
    C   diazepam
    D   chlorambucil
    E   glipizide

2 Mr Taimur is taking alprostadil for erectile dysfunction. Priapism has occurred while taking the medication.
Treatment for this condition should not be delayed for more than how many hours in this patient?

    A   six hours
    B   seven hours
    C   eight hours
    D   nine hours
    E   ten hours

3 Gentamicin is an antibiotic that is regularly used in your hospital. You are asked to update the hospital formulary on the indications for which it can be used.

From the following list, which is NOT a recognised indication for this antibiotic?

    A   biliary tract infection
    B   septicaemia
    C   gonorrhoea
    D   listeral meningitis
    E   neonatal sepsis

4   Dr Ala would like to prescribe enalapril for hypertension for one of his patients. He would like to know the maximum dose that he can give to his patient.
Assuming the patient has no other medical conditions and is not on any other drug therapy, choose the best answer from the list:

    A   5 mg
    B   10 mg
    C   15 mg
    D   20 mg
    E   40 mg

5   You are dispensing a prescription for *Velosef* 250 mg.
What is the generic name of this drug?

    A   ceftazidime
    B   cefradine
    C   cefixime
    D   cefotaxime
    E   cefalexin

6   A consultant on the ward prescribes tacrolimus for a patient who has had a renal transplant.
Which of the following is NOT a side-effect of this drug?

    A   jaundice
    B   tachycardia
    C   dyspnoea
    D   hyperkalaemia
    E   glucose intolerance

7   The rheumatology registrar wishes to initiate penicillamine in one of your patients. She asks you for advice as she is not aware which group of patients should be using this drug with caution.

Choose which condition does NOT require caution with use of this drug:

    A   pregnancy
    B   liver impairment
    C   renal impairment
    D   gold treatment
    E   concomitant nephrotoxic drugs

8   Your local GP wishes to prescribe *Calmurid* cream for one of his patients.
For how many minutes should the patient apply a thick layer of the cream?

    A   one minute
    B   two minutes
    C   four minutes
    D   six minutes
    E   seven minutes

9   A doctor wishes to prescribe malathion lotion for a patient who has scabies on his body and would like the patient to repeat the application after a week.
What total quantity in millilitres should the doctor prescribe?

    A   50 mL
    B   100 mL
    C   150 mL
    D   200 mL
    E   250 mL

10   Mr Bachchan has egg allergy and requires certain vaccines before going on holiday.
Evidence of previous anaphylactic reaction contraindicates which of the following vaccines?

    A   influenza
    B   typhoid
    C   anthrax
    D   diphtheria
    E   hepatitis A

11   A doctor wishes to prescribe an oral typhoid vaccine for his patient.

845

How long after the last dose of vaccine will the patient become protected against typhoid?

    A   1–2 days
    B   2–4 days
    C   4–7 days
    D   7–10 days
    E   11–15 days

12 A patient in an intensive therapy unit has malignant hyperthermia following anaesthesia. The doctors wish to prescribe dantrolene sodium by rapid intravenous injection. The patient weighs 70 kg.
    What initial dose should be prescribed?

    A   35 mg
    B   60 mg
    C   70 mg
    D   90 mg
    E   120 mg

13 A GP wants to prescribe *Premarin* cream for one of her patients. The GP asks you, the pharmacist, to find out how many milligrams per gram (mg/g) of conjugated oestrogens there are in the cream.
    Choose from:

    A   0.625
    B   62.5
    C   625
    D   6250

14 You are a gynaecology pharmacist. The team asks you to suggest suitable hormone replacement therapy (HRT) for a 55-year-old woman, who has an intact uterus. She has no history of any other medical complications, nor is she taking any other medication. She has no allergies.
    Choose the most suitable option for this patient:

    A   *Climaval*
    B   *Elleste-Solo*
    C   *Estraderm TTS*
    D   *Bedol*
    E   *Indivina*

15 A patient on your ward is taking 10 mg of trifluoperazine for schizophrenia daily. You decide with the team that this patient should

be switched to clozapine, as the trifluoperazine does not seem to control the symptoms well. The team asks you to calculate the dose of clozapine equivalent to that of trifluoperazine.

Choose the total daily dose of clozapine equivalent to the patient's dose of trifluoperazine:

    A   50 mg
    B   100 mg
    C   150 mg
    D   200 mg
    E   250 mg

16 From the following options, choose which is NOT a Caution for administering propranolol tablets to a patient:

    A   pregnancy
    B   diabetes
    C   hepatic impairment
    D   insomnia
    E   first-degree atrioventricular block

17 You are on the endocrine team and are reviewing a patient who has diabetes and who is taking metformin. You and your team wish to add rosiglitazone therapy. The patient meets one of the National Institute for Clinical Excellence (NICE) criteria and your team decide to start therapy.

Choose which criteria agree with the NICE guidance 'rosiglitazone for type 2 diabetes mellitus':

    A   patients with poor compliance
    B   patients who are unable to tolerate metformin and gliclazide in combination therapy
    C   patients who have frequent episodes of hypoglycaemia
    D   patients who get frequent sore throats
    E   patients who pay for prescriptions privately

[handwritten annotation: check pioglitazone nice guidelines to see if OB2?]

18 A lady comes to your pharmacy with her prescription. She is a little concerned as she is also breast feeding and is not sure if she should be taking the medications prescribed. She asks for your advice.

Which drug(s) on her prescription would not be suitable for her?

    A   paracetamol
    B   bendroflumethiazide

    C   insulin
    D   erythromycin
    E   latanoprost

19 You are a preregistration pharmacist at a local hospital. You see that a patient has been started on amiodarone. The ward pharmacist explains that this requires monitoring.
Which of the following is NOT a side-effect of amiodarone?

    A   hepatitis
    B   hypothyroidism ✓
    C   hyperthyroidism ✓
    D   taste disturbance ✓
    E   dry mouth

20 Statins are regularly prescribed for patients who have had previous cardiac events. The Committee on Safety for Medicines (CSM) has issued advice for the use of statins.
What effects of the statins has the CSM advised upon?

    A   muscle effects
    B   photosensitivity
    C   blood dyscrasias
    D   serious allergic adverse reactions
    E   pulmonary reactions

21 A patient is taking 10 mg prednisolone tablets once daily. The doctor on the ward wants to change them to hydrocortisone tablets.
What dose of hydrocortisone should the doctor prescribe?

    A   5 mg
    B   10 mg
    C   20 µg
    D   40 mg
    E   60 mg

22 Mrs Clooney visits her GP as she has a persistent dry cough. The GP thinks it may be caused by her medication for hypertension, enalapril. He decides to change it to a suitable alternative.
Which one of the following would be the most suitable?

    A   *Tenormin*
    B   *Hygroton*
    C   *Staril*

D   *Aprovel*
E   *Zestoretic*

23 A GP phones you for advice. He wants to prescribe a 'very potent' topical corticosteroid. The patient is on no other medication.
Which one do you advise?

    A   *Dioderm* cream
    B   *Eumovate* cream
    C   *Diprosalic* ointment
    D   *Dermovate* cream
    E   *Alphaderm* cream

24 A GP phones you. He wants to prescribe some *Betnovate* cream for one of his patients, but is not sure of how much he should prescribe. He wants to prescribe it for six weeks and it is to be used for the patient's legs and trunk twice daily.
How many packs of 100 g of *Betnovate* do you tell the GP to prescribe?

    A   4
    B   8
    C   12
    D   16
    E   32

25 The local GP has prescribed some tadalafil on an FP10 form, for his diabetic patient who has erectile dysfunction.
What must he endorse on the prescription, to authorise the dispensing of the drug?

    A   nothing; the item is blacklisted so cannot be dispensed
    B   Prescriber Contacted
    C   Prescriber Not Contacted
    D   Selected List Scheme
    E   Advisory Committee on Borderline Substances

26 Mrs Tammworth has recently been prescribed hormone replacement therapy. She is concerned about the side-effects of HRT and would like you to give her more information. During your discussion, you mention side-effects that may occur, in which case she should stop her HRT immediately.
Which of the following is NOT a reason to stop treatment with HRT?

A severe stomach pain
B severe chest pain
C cough with blood-stained sputum
D sore throat or flu-like symptoms
E prolonged headache

27 You have a patient on your ward who is prescribed fluids for parenteral feeding. The nutrition team prescribe *Clinimix N14G30E* 1 litre bag. How many millimoles of magnesium ions per litre does this bag contain?

A 2.0
B 2.5
C 3.0
D 3.5
E 4.0

28 A GP phones you at your pharmacy for some advice. He is prescribing some *Eumovate* cream for one of his adult patients for the trunk area. The GP would like to prescribe four weeks supply for a once-daily application.
How many grams of *Eumovate* should the GP prescribe?

A 15 g
B 30 g
C 100 g
D 200 g
E 400 g

29 Which of the following preparations is considered by the Joint Formulary Committee to be less suitable for prescribing?

A digoxin
B interferon alfa
C treosulfan
D chlorpropamide
E co-cyprindiol

30 Mr Burkhart is a 52-year-old contractor who normally pays for his prescription. He presents a prescription as follows:
warfarin 5 mg 1 od
warfarin 3 mg 1 od
warfarin 1 mg 2 od

How many charges do you take?

    A   no charge
    B   one charge
    C   two charges
    D   three charges
    E   four charges

31 A cardiac house officer asks your advice on what oral loading dose of amiodarone can be given to a patient with atrial fibrillation who will then be maintained on a dose of 200 mg daily. You can assume that amiodarone is appropriate for this patient, and that the patient has no renal or liver failure.
What advice do you give?

    A   600 mg stat then 200 mg daily
    B   200 mg tds for seven days then 200 mg bd for seven days then 200 mg od thereafter
    C   200 mg tds for one day then 200 mg bd for one day then 200 mg od thereafter
    D   100 mg tds for seven days then 100 mg bd for seven days then 200 mg od thereafter
    E   600 mg tds for seven days then 400 mg for seven days then 200 mg od thereafter

32 The pain sister asks for your advice. A patient on the ward has been receiving morphine sulphate 60 mg tablets every four hours. She would like to change over to morphine sulphate subcutaneous infusion every 24 hours.
What daily dose of morphine sulphate subcutaneous infusion would be equivalent to the patient's oral daily dose?

    A   30 mg
    B   60 mg
    C   90 mg
    D   120 mg
    E   180 mg

33 A GP phones you for advice. She has a patient who normally takes prednisolone tablets 30 mg twice daily for ulcerative colitis. The GP would like to change the choice of steroid to dexamethasone.
What total daily dose of dexamethasone would be equivalent to the patient's current prednisolone regimen?

A   0.75 mg
B   1 mg
C   3 mg
D   4 mg
E   9 mg

34   Mrs Ghouti comes to your pharmacy complaining that she has been constipated for three days. She tells you that she has recently started taking ferrous sulphate (dried) 200 mg tablets three times daily. She would like an alternative iron salt, but she insists that it should have the same content of ferrous iron as the ferrous sulphate (dried) tablets. Which of the following regimens do you recommend?

A   ferrous fumarate 200 mg three times a day
B   ferrous gluconate 300 mg three times a day
C   ferrous succinate 100 mg three times a day
D   ferrous sulphate 200 mg three times a day
E   ferrous sulphate (dried) 100 mg three times a day

35   You are on call and one of the ward sisters pages you to find out which infusion fluid to use with *DaunoXome* and what is the recommended method of infusion.
What do you recommend?

A   intermittent infusion in glucose 10%
B   intermittent infusion in glucose 5%
C   intermittent infusion in sodium chloride 0.9%
D   continuous infusion in glucose 5%
E   continuous infusion in sodium chloride 0.9%

36   Mrs Ghatoor is taking phenelzine for depression.
Which of the following does NOT interact with this drug?

A   alcohol
B   clonidine
C   nicorandil
D   piroxicam
E   tetrabenazine

37   A patient on your ward has just been started on erythromycin tablets for an infection. You check for interactions on his prescription chart. Which of the following drugs from his prescription does NOT interact with erythromycin?

A   darifenacin
B   reboxetine
C   atenolol
D   simvastatin
E   methylprednisolone

38 Mr Stone has returned to your pharmacy some fentanyl patches which he no longer uses. The Royal Pharmaceutical Society inspector is coincidentally visiting your premises that day and offers to be your witness for the destruction of the patches.
What would be the most appropriate method for the destruction of the patches?

A   add to cat litter
B   place it in a small amount of soapy water
C   throw in the 'sharps' bin
D   remove the backing and fold patch over upon itself
E   tear the patch in four and throw in a special bin

39 Which of the following is NOT a contraindication for *Yasmin* tablets?

A   migraine with typical focal aura
B   pregnancy
C   mild renal impairment
D   liver disease
E   breast cancer

40 Mr Zaman is a 42-year-old, non-diabetic, non-smoker. His average blood pressure is 180/94 mmHg. His serum total cholesterol to HDL cholesterol ratio is 8.
What is his cardiovascular risk prediction over the next 10 years?

A   <15%
B   >15%
C   10–20%
D   >20%
E   >30%

41 A prescription is brought to your pharmacy for *Naramig*. You wish to check the generic name for this drug so that you can check the dose, and check for any interactions with any of the customer's current medication.
What is the approved name of the medicine on the prescription?

A sumatriptan
B zolmitriptan
C pizotifen
D naratriptan
E almotriptan

42 A child is due for their MMR vaccine. The outpatients' clinic telephones you to confirm its appropriateness for the child.
Which of the following from the list is NOT contraindicated for the use of the MMR vaccine?

A children with allergy to gelatin
B children who have received a live vaccine injection eight weeks ago
C children taking ciclosporin
D children allergic to neomycin
E children who have had a *Vigam* injection within the past three months

43 A doctor wishes to prescribe some ribavirin capsules. He asks you to suggest a dose for his patient, who weighs 69 kg.
Assuming that the patient has 'normal' renal function, what dose regimen do you recommend?

A 600 mg twice daily
B 600 mg in the morning and 200 mg in the evening
C 400 mg twice daily
D 400 mg in the morning and 600 mg in the evening
E 200 mg in the morning and 400 mg in the evening

44 From the list, which is not a general sale list medicine?
A damiana
B emedastine
C *Oilatum* cream
D *Otodex*
E *Eurax*

45 Mrs Quinn is a 55-year-old lady who normally pays for her prescriptions. She presents with a prescription for the following items:

Prempak-C 1 OP
Naproxen 250 mg 28

How many NHS prescription charges do you take for this prescription?

A none
B two
C three
D four
E five

46 Miss Yousaf normally pays for her prescriptions. She is 23 years old and is a dentist.
She presents a prescription to you for the following:

Cilest tablets
mefenamic acid tablets
tranexamic acid tablets

How many NHS prescription charges do you take for this prescription?

A none
B one
C two
D three
E four

47 A pregnant woman, who is in her third trimester, asks for some pain relief, as she has had a painful back since last night. She is not allergic to anything.
What would be the safest analgesic for her?

A *Cuprofen*
B *Paracodol*
C *Nurofen Plus*
D *Ibuleve* gel
E *Panadol*

48 Ms Desor is a 26-year-old woman who is in anaphylactic shock caused by peanuts.
Which dose of intramuscular adrenaline (epinephrine) would be most suitable for her?

A 50 µg
B 100 µg
C 120 µg
D 250 µg
E 500 µg

49 Mr Agrawal comes to your pharmacy complaining of a sore throat and fever. He would like you to recommend appropriate therapy. You check his patient medication record (PMR) and find that one of his drugs is likely to cause flu-like symptoms and you immediately refer him to the accident and emergency unit.
Which of the following drugs from his PMR causes concern?

   A   carbimazole
   B   naproxen
   C   perindopril
   D   pravastatin
   E   hydrocortisone ointment

50 Which of the following chemotherapy drugs may be administered intrathecally?

   A   vinblastine
   B   vincristine
   C   methotrexate
   D   vindesine
   E   vinorelbine

51 Mr Chauhan has glucose-6-phosphate dehydrogenase deficiency.
Which of the following drugs would have a POSSIBLE risk of haemolysis?

   A   primaquine
   B   ciprofloxacin
   C   nitrofurantoin
   D   quinidine
   E   dapsone

52 Mrs Munir comes to your pharmacy for some advice. She has been told in a recent allergy test that she is allergic to tartrazine, and that this is an 'E' number. She would like you to find out which one.
Which one of the following numbers is used for tartrazine?

   A   E102
   B   E171
   C   E422
   D   E124
   E   E132

53 A patient presents a prescription for nabilone. You have never seen this drug before and wish to check the indication.
Which of the following is the correct indication for this drug?

    A   pain
    B   pyrexia
    C   nausea
    D   mania
    E   depression

54 Miss Ravalia pays for her prescriptions. She is 23 years old and is a physiotherapist. She presents a prescription to you for the following:
TriNovum tablets 1 OP

piroxicam capsules 20 mg 1 OP

How many NHS charges would be levied for these items?

    A   none
    B   one
    C   two
    D   three
    E   four

The answers for this section are on pp 39–46.

MULTIPLE COMPLETION QUESTIONS

Each one of the questions or incomplete statements in this section is followed by three responses. For each question, ONE or MORE of the responses is/are correct. Decide which of the responses is/are correct, then choose:

A   if 1, 2, and 3 are correct
B   if 1 and 2 only are correct
C   if 2 and 3 only are correct
D   if 1 only is correct
E   if 3 only is correct

Directions summarised:

A	B	C	D	E
1, 2, 3	1, 2 only	2, 3 only	1 only	3 only

1   A lady comes into your pharmacy for some advice. She normally takes *Microgynon* everyday at 9 p.m. She is in the middle of her cycle and forgot to take her pill last night and is not sure what she should do. Given that it is 11 a.m. when she comes to see you, what advice do you give?

   1   Take a pill straight away, then take the next one at her normal time
   2   She must use condoms for the next seven days or abstain from sex
   3   Miss out the seven inactive pills for the following month

2   You are on call and the sister on one of the wards asks for your advice. She has different ferric complexes on the ward, but is not sure which one(s) she can give parenterally. What advice do you give about the following?

   1   iron dextran
   2   iron sucrose
   3   iron sorbitol

3   Mrs Floyd is a regular customer in your community pharmacy. She asks to speak to you as she has started to feel very depressed since her husband's death. She shows you an article that she has read in a

women's magazine about St John's wort. She would like to try it but would like your advice. You consult her patient medical record and tell her that St John's wort would not be appropriate for her as it would not 'work well' with her regular medications.

Which of the following drugs from her PMR should be avoided with St John's wort?

1 aripiprazole
2 simvastatin
3 carbamazepine

4 Mr Gunn asks for some advice on malaria prophylaxis. He is going to Pakistan for his holidays and will be spending four weeks there. His flight is in nine days time.

Which of the following regimens do you recommend?

1 doxycycline 100 mg od
  total quantity 58 capsules
2 chloroquine 300 mg (base) once weekly
  total quantity 10 tablets
3 proguanil 200 mg od
  total quantity 62 tablets

5 A man comes to the pharmacy asking for the 'morning after pill' for his girlfriend. They had unprotected sex 24 hours ago and his girlfriend is on no other medicines.

You decide not to supply it because:

1 emergency contraception is not available without a prescription
2 emergency contraception is not effective within 24 hours of unprotected sex
3 you have to interview his girlfriend personally, unless it is an exceptional circumstance

6 The use of fluted bottles is legally required if the following are sold or supplied:

1 oil of croton
2 hydrofluoric acid
3 atropine sulphate eye drops

7 You have ordered some zinc phosphide for the destruction of rats and mice.

How should you store this so that it meets legal requirements?

1   in a cupboard or drawer reserved solely for the storage of poisons
2   on a shelf reserved solely for poisons
3   in the household section with 'other' rat and mice killers

8   Which is true, regarding the sale and supply of strychnine?

1   It must be supplied in original packaging
2   You can only be supplied in units of up to 2 g
3   Agriculturists do not need authorisation for its purchase

9   The sister on your ward asks for some advice for one of the terminally ill patients. A syringe driver needs to be set up with diamorphine subcutaneously. The doctors have prescribed some other drugs which are also to be added to the syringe driver.
    Which of the following drug(s) is/are compatible with diamorphine?

1   haloperidol
2   midazolam
3   hyoscine butylbromide

10 A patient presents a prescription to the pharmacy.
    Which of the following are not prescribable under the NHS?

1   *Ucerax*
2   *Otrivine* nose drops
3   hypromellose eye drops

11 A patient presents a FP10D to you.
    Which of the below CANNOT be prescribed on this type of form?

1   nystatin ointment
2   doxycycline capsules
3   ciprofloxacin

12 You have a woman on your gynaecology ward for whom the doctor wants to prescribe an HRT preparation. The patient had a hysterectomy about one year ago.
    Which preparation(s) would be suited to her?

1   *Elleste-Solo* tablets
2   *Progynova*
3   *Premique*

13 A concerned lady comes to your pharmacy and gives you a list of drugs which her GP has just prescribed for her. She forgot to tell her GP that she is still breast feeding her baby.
Which drugs from her prescription should she avoid?

1 metformin
2 phentolamine
3 tolterodine

14 Mr Iver is a patient on your ward with *severe* liver disease. Which of the drugs from the list below should be AVOIDED in this group of patients?

1 diclofenac
2 iron sucrose
3 atorvastatin

15 One of your patients has been prescribed some finasteride tablets for his male-pattern baldness. He lives with his wife and three children. Which of the following is NOT a counselling point for this drug?

1 Use of condoms are recommended if partner is likely to become or is pregnant
2 Women of childbearing potential should avoid handling broken tablets
3 Avoid exposure to sunlight as photosensitive reactions may occur

16 Which of the following drugs may cause blood disorders?

1 methotrexate
2 vancomycin
3 ganciclovir

17 Which of the following is/are non-medicinal poisons?

1 *Metastron*
2 arsenic tribromide
3 magnesium phosphide

18 Which of the following liquids for external use require to be sold or supplied in a fluted bottle, by legislation?

1 adrenaline (epinephrine)
2 demecarium bromide
3 carbachol

19 You have just received some oxycodone tablets from your wholesaler. What information do you record in the Controlled Drugs register?

1   date on which order was submitted
2   form in which drug received
3   amount received

20 Emergency supply at the request of the patient cannot be given if the prescription-only medicine contains which of the following substances:

1   calcium bromide
2   potassium bromide
3   sodium bromide

21 From the following list, choose which substance(s) can be administered parenterally by a registered midwife:

1   phytomenadione
2   diamorphine
3   naloxone hydrochloride

22 A GP telephones asking for some advice. He wants to withdraw prednisolone tablets from one of his patients. The Committee on Safety of Medicines (CSM) advises that gradual withdrawal should be considered in those whose disease is unlikely to relapse and

1   in patients who have recently received repeated courses
2   in patients who have received more than 40 mg daily of prednisolone
3   in patients who have received more than three weeks' treatment

23 Mr Carlos is a patient on your ward with rheumatoid arthritis. He has been prescribed auranofin for active progressive rheumatoid arthritis. What are the main side-effects of this drug?

1   paraesthesia
2   cholestatic jaundice
3   metallic taste

24 You are working with the Macmillan palliative care team in your hospital. One of the doctors asks you to recommend something for one of her patients who has hiccups.
Which of the following would be appropriate to recommend?

1 chlorphenamine
2 methadone
3 baclofen

25 Some Latin abbreviations are used in prescribing. Which of the following abbreviations match with the correct translation?

1 a.c = ante cibum
2 t.i.d = ter in die
3 o.m = omni mane

26 A doctor wants to prescribe teriparatide for one of his patients and asks you if it is safe for this patient. From the following, in which group(s) of patients is this drug contraindicated?

1 Paget's disease
2 the elderly
3 patients with a history of alcohol abuse

27 Mrs Springer is currently on hormone replacement therapy. Which of the following is/are contraindications?

1 deep vein thrombosis
2 liver disease
3 breastfeeding

28 Sildenafil can be prescribed under the NHS under certain circumstances. It can be prescribed to treat erectile dysfunction in men who:

1 have hypertension
2 have liver problems
3 have multiple sclerosis

29 A woman has just been started on *TriNovum* tablets. You counsel her about the medication and advise her under what circumstances she should stop treatment.
Which symptom(s) should prompt her to stop treatment immediately?

1 sudden breathlessness
2 severe stomach pain
3 breast tenderness

30 You are working for the medicines information department in your hospital. The obstetrics senior house officer telephones to ask your

advice. He has a pregnant patient who is diabetic. He would like to know the most appropriate antidiabetic medication for her.
Which of the following would be appropriate for her?

1   insulin
2   metformin
3   gliclazide

31 One of the doctors in obstetrics asks you about midwives administering drugs.
Which of the following can midwives not administer parenterally?

1   oxytocin
2   pethidine
3   omeprazole

32 You would like to set up a repeat medication service in your pharmacy.
With which of the following professional standards should you comply?

1   The request for the service must come from the patient
2   Your pharmacy must operate a patient medication record
3   Records of all interventions should be kept

33 For the past few days, one of the patients on your ward has had erratic blood glucose levels.
Which of the following drug(s) is/are likely to be the cause?

1   *Denzapine*
2   bumetanide
3   pantoprazole

34 Mrs Sahota is one of your regular customers. She brings in a prescription for *Fosamax*. She has never had these tablets before. You counsel her on the new tablets. Which points are specific to this drug?

1   swallow whole
2   do not take the tablets at bedtime or before rising
3   these tablets may cause drowsiness

35 A senior registrar in obstetrics wants to prescribe dinoprostone to induce labour in one of his patients. He contacts you to check whether this drug is contraindicated in his patient.
In which of the following circumstances is this drug contraindicated?

1 patients with a history of caesarean section
2 patients with renal disease
3 patients who have had unexplained bleeding during pregnancy

36 A child has been rushed to the accident and emergency unit, as she has been stung by a wasp and is experiencing anaphylactic shock.
Which of her symptoms requires immediate treatment?

1 shaking/tremor
2 hypotension
3 bronchospasm

37 Which of the following is/are true regarding glucose-6-phosphate dehydrogenase deficiency?

1 Moth balls may cause haemolysis in these individuals
2 The risk and severity of haemolysis due to taking a drug is almost always dose related
3 The deficiency is prevalent in individuals originating from southern Europe

38 According to the CRM guidelines on handling cytotoxic drugs, which of the following is/are true?

1 Pregnant staff should not handle cytotoxics
2 The eyes should be protected
3 Only trained individuals should reconstitute cytotoxics

39 One of your patients on the ward has recently developed severe hyponatraemia. You check the drug chart to see if any of his drugs may be the cause.
Which of the following drug(s) may cause hyponatraemia?

1 propranolol
2 bumetanide
3 fluoxetine

40 A patient on your ward has severe renal impairment.
Which drugs should be avoided?

1 buspirone
2 ropinirole
3 tinzaparin

41 Mr Kudhail has alcoholic liver cirrhosis. Which of the following drugs is/are to be avoided in liver impairment?

1 piperazine
2 methysergide
3 medroxyprogesterone

42 Mrs Brocchini has been prescribed atenolol for hypertension. She would like to know the formulations available for this drug.
In which of the following formulations can atenolol NOT be given?

1 tablet
2 liquid
3 suppositories

43 Which of the following are suitable for the treatment of an acute gout attack?

1 indometacin
2 colchicine
3 allopurinol

44 Which of the following can be given in liver impairment?

1 leflunomide
2 vinblastine
3 atomoxetine

45 Miss Modha's GP has prescribed *Trimovate* cream for her eczema. She asks you about the side-effects.
Which of the below is/are a side-effect of the cream?

1 contact dermatitis
2 thinning of the skin
3 acne

46 Ms Popat is in her second trimester of pregnancy.
Which of the following drugs is/are to be AVOIDED in this trimester?

1 enoxaparin
2 methyldopa
3 ciprofloxacin

47 Which person(s) is/are authorised to supervise the destruction of controlled drugs?

1 Home Office inspector
2 Royal Pharmaceutical Society inspector
3 Registered General Medical Council doctor

48 Which of the following substances, if contained in oral liquid preparations, are exempt from controlled-drugs safe-custody requirements?

1 pipradrol
2 fenethylline
3 methylphenidate

49 Which of the following drugs can be given as an emergency supply at the request of a patient? (Assume that you have interviewed the patient, that there is a genuine need for the drug and that the patient has had it before).

1 fentanyl patches
2 temazepam tablets
3 oxybutynin tablets

50 You do NOT dispense this prescription (see p. 26) because:

1 the prescription is not in the prescriber's own handwriting
2 the total quantity is not in words
3 the directions for use are not on the prescription

51 A patient presents the following prescription (see p. 27) to you. You decide not to dispense it because:

1 the total quantity in words in missing
2 the patient's date of birth is missing
3 the patients address is missing

52 Regarding keeping records of controlled drugs:

1 controlled drug registers may NOT be kept on a computer
2 the author of each entry should be identifiable
3 records must be preserved for two years

53 The following controlled drugs may be prescribed by a nurse independent prescriber for palliative care:

1 lorazepam
2 diamorphine
3 midazolam

Pharmacy Stamp	Age **29** D.o.B. **10/10/77**	Name (including forename) and address Michael Lamphard 49 Brockfield Gds E24	
Number of days' treatment N.B. Ensure dose is stated			

Endorsements
 	
    Secobarbital 50mg tablets
 	
    Total quantity 28
			Office use

Signature of Doctor *Nadia Bukhari*		Date 30.6.07	
For dispenser No. of Persons on form	**Dr N. Bukhari** **45 Handel House WC1** **Brunswick Green PCT** **97865430** **Tel: 020 7222 2222**		FP10 CD
NHS	PATIENTS – please read the notes overleaf		

Assume today's date is 2.7.07

Pharmacy Stamp	Age **26** D.o.B.		Name (including forename) and address Andrew Herbert	
Number of days' treatment N.B. Ensure dose is stated				
Endorsements		Temazepam 10mg One daily Total quantity 56		Office use
Signature of Doctor *Nadia Bukhari*			Date 16.9.07	
For dispenser No. of Persons on form	**Dr N. Bukhari** **45 Handel House WC1** **Brunswick Green PCT** **97865430** **Tel: 020 7222 2222**			FP10 CD

Assume today's date is 20.9.07

54 Which of the following poisons no longer have approval from the Pesticides Safety Directorate?

1 zinc phosphide
2 potassium cyanide
3 sodium arsenite

55 Signed orders of Schedule 1 poisons must state:

1 the signature of the purchaser
2 his/her trade
3 the date

56 Which person(s) from the following list is/are permitted to supply or administer under patient group directions?

1 pharmacists
2 dentists
3 doctors

The answers for this section are on pp 47–53.

CLASSIFICATION QUESTIONS

For each numbered question, select the one lettered option that most closely corresponds to the answer. Within each group of questions each lettered option may be used once, more than once, or not at all.

What are names for the following E numbers?

1 E420
2 E171
3 E142
4 E104

    A quinoline yellow
    B sorbitol
    C green S
    D amaranth
    E titanium dioxide

Which of the following are known to potentially interact with:

5 lithium?
6 metoclopramide?
7 omeprazole?
8 allopurinol?

    A phenytoin
    B linezolid
    C propranolol
    D ciclosporin
    E amlodipine

On your ward, you have come across some drugs that you do not recognise. You want to find out what their indications are.

Match the indications with the drugs.

9 control of intra-ocular pressure
10 anaemia associated with chronic renal failure
11 moderate to severe pain
12 prevention of spina bifida in pregnancy

A   apraclonidine
B   paracetamol
C   epoetin alfa
D   folic acid
E   buprenorphine

Match the correct cautionary labels with the following drugs:

13   co-danthramer
14   *Pariet*
15   levetiracetam
16   *Tenormin*

A   Do not stop taking this medicine except on your doctor's advice
B   Swallowed whole, not chewed
C   Dissolve or mix with water before taking
D   Warning: may cause drowsiness
E   This medicine may colour urine

Which of the following drugs:

17   is used for the induction of labour?
18   is used to treat hypoglycaemia?
19   may cause haemolytic anaemia in individuals deficient in glucose-6-phosphate dehydrogenase?
20   is used as first-line treatment in overweight, diabetic patients?

A   oxybutynin
B   oxytocin
C   nitrofurantoin
D   metformin
E   glucagon

Which of the following drugs:

21   is contraindicated in phaeochromocytoma?
22   raises prolactin concentration?
23   has a narrow therapeutic range?
24   can be used for nausea and vomiting?

A   theophylline
B   nitrazepam
C   domperidone
D   betahistine
E   vigabatrin

Which of the following drugs:

25 is used for the treatment of anaphylaxis?
26 is contraindicated in patients who have had a recent myocardial infarction?
27 causes testicular enlargement as a side-effect?
28 is used to treat acromegaly?

 A adrenaline (epinephrine)
 B ispaghula
 C simvastatin
 D amitriptyline
 E octreotide

Miss B is a regular customer at your pharmacy. She normally pays for her prescriptions.
How many NHS charges would be levied for the following items?

29 *Femodette* 1 OP
30 *Scholl* stockings class II × 2 pairs
31 paracetamol 500 mg tabs × 112
32 carbamazepine 300 mg tabs 3 OP

 A none
 B one
 C two
 D three
 E four

Which of the following from the list of drugs provided:

33 may be given on emergency supply?
34 is a Schedule 1 controlled drug?
35 can be used in the treatment of epilepsy?
36 is a controlled drug EXEMPT from safe-custody requirement?

 A temazepam tablets
 B *MST Continus* tablets
 C pregabalin
 D quinalbarbitone
 E cannabis

Which of the following:

37 can be used for the treatment of neuropathic pain?

38 can be used for the treatment of peripheral vascular disease?
39 can be used for the treatment of hypertensive crisis?
40 can be used for the short-term relief of muscle spasm?

    A   gabapentin
    B   sodium nitroprusside
    C   carisoprodol
    D   inositol nicotinate
    E   tizanidine

From the following list, select which drug:

41 interacts with ibuprofen
42 may cause polydipsia
43 may be used to treat obstructive sleep apnoea syndrome
44 may cause ototoxicity

    A   lithium
    B   aztreonam
    C   amikacin
    D   modafinil
    E   betahistine

Match the following controlled drugs to the correct schedule:

45 temazepam
46 quinalbarbitone
47 co-codaprin
48 hexobarbitone sodium

    A   Schedule 1
    B   Schedule 2
    C   Schedule 3
    D   Schedule 4
    E   Schedule 5

Match the side-effect with the following drugs:

49 anagrelide
50 potassium chloride
51 methotrexate
52 sodium oxybate

    A   folate deficiency
    B   asthenia

C   congestive heart failure
D   disturbance in colour vision
E   heart toxicity

Match the interaction with the pairs of drugs:

53   zidovudine + ganciclovir
54   ciclosporin + saquinavir
55   venlafaxine + warfarin
56   methyldopa + torasemide

A   enhanced hypotensive effect
B   enhanced anticoagulant effect
C   plasma concentration of both drugs increased
D   toxicity of the narrow therapeutic drug
E   profound myelosuppression

Which of the following:

57   is used for the treatment of urticaria?
58   is not prescribable on the NHS?
59   has been deemed less suitable for prescribing by the Joint Formulary
     Committee?
60   is contraindicated in patients with hypersensitivity to triprolidine?

A   *Medix Lifecare Nebuliser System*
B   guanethidine monosulphate
C   acrivastine
D   *Pocket Chamber*
E   standard peak flow meter

The answers for this section are on pp 54–58.

STATEMENT QUESTIONS

The following questions consist of a statement in the top row followed by a second statement beneath.

Decide whether the **first statement** is true or false.

Decide whether the **second statement** is true or false.

Then choose:

A   if both statements are true and the second statement is a correct explanation of the first statement

B   if both statements are true but the second statement is NOT a correct explanation of the first statement

C   if the first statement is true but the second statement is false

D   if the first statement is false but the second statement is true

E   if both statements are false

1   **First statement**

Gastrocote tablets should be used with caution in diabetic patients with dyspepsia

Second statement

Gastrocote tablets have a high sugar content

2   **First statement**

All H_2-receptor antagonists heal gastric and duodenal ulcers

Second statement

H_2-antagonists reduce gastric acid output as a result of histamine H_2-receptor blockade

3   **First statement**

Ivabradine is a drug that lowers heart rate

Second statement

Ivabradine acts on the bundle of His

4 **First statement**

Atypical antipsychotics should be considered when choosing first-line treatment of newly diagnosed schizophrenia

Second statement

Olanzapine is associated with an increased risk of stroke in elderly patients with dementia

5 **First statement**

Nausea in the first trimester of pregnancy is usually mild

Second statement

Metoclopramide should be given as first-line treatment for mild nausea in pregnancy

6 **First statement**

Pethidine should be avoided in patients with sickle-cell disease

Second statement

Pethidine can precipitate gout

7 **First statement**

Potassium should be monitored in patients prescribed ciclosporin therapy

Second statement

Ciclosporin may cause hyperkalaemia

8 **First statement**

Peptac liquid is suitable for patients with dyspepsia who also have hypertension

Second statement

Peptac liquid is a low-sodium preparation

9 **First statement**

Patients taking dopaminergic drugs should exercise caution when driving

Second statement

Doperminergic drugs can cause a sudden onset of sleep at any time during the day or night

10 **First statement**

Mifepristone is used for the induction of labour in normal pregnancy

Second statement

Mifepristone sensitises the myometrium to prostaglandin-induced contractions and ripens the cervix

11 **First statement**

Diabetic ketoacidosis may induce hyponatraemia

Second statement

Sodium chloride in isotonic solution is indicated for hyponatraemia induced by diabetic ketoacidosis

12 **First statement**

Vitamin C deficiency causes rickets

Second statement

Vitamin C is a fat-soluble vitamin

13 **First statement**

Penicillamine is used for the treatment of Wilson's disease

Second statement

Penicillamine aids the elimination of magnesium ions

14 **First statement**

Artificial saliva can be prescribed for patients with a dry mouth

Second statement

Tricyclic antidepressants can cause dry mouth

15 **First statement**

Patients taking methotrexate should report signs of infection, especially sore throat

Second statement

Methotrexate therapy may induce agranulocystosis

16 **First statement**

Amprenavir interacts with St John's wort

Second statement

St John's wort reduces the concentration of amprenavir

17 **First statement**

Ganciclovir can be given safely in pregnancy

Second statement

Ganciclovir does not cross the placenta

The answers for this section are on pp 59–61.

Open book answers

SIMPLE COMPLETION ANSWERS

1 E

Acute porphyrias are hereditary disorders. There are four types: acute intermittent, variegate, hereditary coproporphyria and 5-aminolaevulinic acid dehydratase deficiency. A defect in haem metabolism, owing to a specific enzyme deficiency, causes porphyrins to accumulate.

Care must be taken when prescribing for these patients, as many drugs can precipate acute porphyria crises. The patient would have severe abdominal pain, which can also radiate to the back and thighs. Confusion can also occur in some patients.

Chapter 9 (Nutrition and Blood) of the *British National Formulary* (BNF), has a table of unsafe drugs and drug groups in these patients.

2 A

Priapism is a long painful erection and can last from a few hours to a couple of days. This type of erection is not associated with sexual desires or sexual activity. It is caused by a disruption of blood flow to the penis shaft. The blood usually gets trapped in the erection chambers, prolonging the erection. Priapism can be drug related, and in this case alprostadil is the likely cause.

3 C

This information can be found in the BNF, Chapter 5 (Infections), under Gentamicin. Gentamicin can be used for the following main indications: septicaemia, neonatal sepsis, meningitis and other CNS infections, biliary-tract infection, acute pyelonephritis or prostatitis, endocarditis and pneumonia (hospital patients only), and it is used as an adjunct in listerial meningitis.

4 E
This information can be found in the BNF, Chapter 2 (Cardiovascular system), under Enalapril maleate. The maximum dose of enalapril is 40 mg, once daily.

5 B
This information can be found in the BNF, Chapter 5 (Infections), in the cephalosporins section, under Cefradine.

6 E
Alopecia is not a side-effect of this drug. All the other side-effects are listed in the BNF, Chapter 8 (Malignant disease and immunosuppression), in section 8.2.2, under Tacrolimus.

7 B
Liver impairment is not a caution for use of penicillamine. This information can be found in the BNF, Chapter 10 (Musculoskeletal and joint disease).

8 C
BNF Chapter 13 (Skin), under the dose for *Calmurid*, it states: 'For dry, scaling and itchy skin, apply a thick layer for 3–5 minutes'.

9 D
BNF Chapter 13 (Skin); table 'Suitable quantities of parasiticidal preparations to be prescribed for specific areas of the body'. For a single application for scabies, 100 mL of lotion is required. Therefore, if the doctor wants the patient to repeat the application, the total quantity will be 200 mL.

10 A
BNF Chapter 14 (Immunological products and vaccines). Under Active immunity, it states that: 'Hypersensitivity to egg with evidence of previous anaphylactic reaction, contra-indicates influenza vaccine, tick-borne encephalitis vaccine and yellow fever vaccine.'

11 D
BNF Chapter 14 (Immunological products and vaccines). Under Typhoid vaccines', it states that: 'An oral vaccine can be taken as three doses of one capsule on alternate days, providing protection 7–10 days after the last dose'.

12 C
BNF Chapter 15 (Anaesthesia), under the subheading Drugs for malignant hyperthermia. The dose required is 1 mg/kg initially. The patient weighs 70 kg; therefore the dose is 70 mg.

13 A
BNF Chapter 7 (Obstetrics, gynaecology and urinary tract disorders), section 7.2.1, *Premarin* cream contains 625 µg per gram of conjugated oestrogens. Therefore, in milligrams, divide by 1000 = 0.625 mg/g.

14 E
BNF Chapter 6 (Endocrine system). Section 6.4.1.1 states that 'A woman with an intact uterus normally requires oestrogen with cyclical progesterone' and 'An oestrogen alone is suitable for continous use in women without a uterus'.

15 B
BNF Chapter 4 (Central nervous system). There is a table in section 4.2.1 'Equivalent doses of oral antipsychotics', which states that 5 mg of trifluoperazine = 50 mg of clozapine. Therefore, 10 mg of trifluoperazine = 100 mg of clozapine.

16 D
BNF Chapter 2 (Cardiovascular system) under Propranolol. The cautions are listed and insomnia is not one of them.

17 B
BNF Chapter 6 (Endocrine system). NICE guidance in section 6.1.2.3 states: 'NICE has advised that the use of rosiglitazone as second-line therapy added to metformin is not recommended, except for patients who are unable to tolerate metformin with a sulphonylurea in combination therapy, or patients in whom metformin or sulphonylurea is contraindicated.'

18 E
The answer for this can be found in BNF, Appendix 5 (Breast-feeding). For the list of drugs given, only latanoprost is to be avoided in breast feeding.

19 E
BNF Chapter 2 (Cardiovascular systems). Patients taking amiodarone can

develop corneal microdeposits, phototoxic reactions and disorders of thyroid function (amiodarone contains iodine). Amiodarone is also associated with hepatotoxicity and treatment should be discontinued if severe liver function abnormalities develop. Taste disturbance is also a reported side-effect for this drug.

20 A
BNF Chapter 2 (Cardiovascular system). The CSM has advised that rhabdomyolysis is associated with lipid-regulating drugs.

21 D
BNF Chapter 6 (Endocrine disorders); section 6.3.2. Equivalent anti-inflammatory doses of corticosteroids.
5 mg of prednisolone = 20 mg of hydrocortisone.
10 mg prednisolone = 20 × 2 = 40 mg of hydrocortisone.

22 D
BNF Cardiovascular systems (Chapter 2).
Losartan is an angiotensin II receptor antagonist and it has properties similar to ACE inhibitors, but it does not inhibit the breakdown of brady-kinin, and thus does not cause the persistent dry cough.
Angiotensin II receptor antagonists are a good alternative for patients on ACE inhibitors who have the dry cough.
Aprovel is the brand name for losartan.

23 D
BNF Chapter 13 (Skin); section 13.4 Topical corticosteroid preparation potencies.

24 C
BNF Chapter 13 (Skin); section 13.4 Suitable quantities of topical corticosteroid preparation to be prescribed for specific areas of the body.
Amount of cream for both legs and trunk area is 200 g for a once-daily application for two weeks; therefore for twice daily application for two weeks, 200 × 2 = 400 g is required. Therefore for six weeks you need 400 × 3 = 1200 g.
The tubes come in 100 g packs therefore you need 1200/100 = 12 packs.

25 D
Drug treatment for erectile dysfunction may only be prescribed on the NHS under certain circumstances. The prescriber has to endorse the prescription with a 'SLS'. Diabetes is a condition where treatment for erectile dysfunction can be prescribed on the NHS.

26 D
BNF Chapter 7 (Obstetrics, gynecology, and urinary-tract disorders); section 7.3.1 Reason to stop immediately.
    Hormone replacement therapy should be stopped if any of the following occur: sudden severe chest pain, sudden breathlessness, unexplained severe pain in calf of one leg, severe stomach pain, serious neurological effects, liver disease, blood pressure above systolic 160 mmHg and diastolic 100 mmHg, prolonged immobility after surgery or leg injury and detection of a risk factor which contra-indicates treatment.

27 B
BNF Chapter 9 (Nutrition and blood); section 9.3 Proprietary Infusion Fluids for Parenteral Feeding.

28 D
BNF Chapter 13 (Skin); section 13.4 'Suitable quantities of corticosteroid preparations to be prescribed for specific areas of the body'.

29 D
BNF Chapter 6 (Endocrine system).
    Chlorpropamide has more side-effects than other sulphonylureas because of its very prolonged duration of action and the consequent hazard of hypoglycemia; therefore it is not recommended for use.

30 B
Drugs prescribed in more than one strength with the same formulation are classed as one NHS charge.

31 B
BNF Chapter 2 (Cardiovascular system).
    Amiodarone has a very long halflife, thus patients need a loading dose when initiating treatment: 200 mg three times daily for seven days then 200 mg twice daily for seven days then 200 mg once daily maintenance.

32 E
BNF Prescribing in palliative care; table 'Equivalent doses of morphine sulphate by mouth or subcutaneous infusion'

33 E
BNF Chapter 6 (Endocrine system); section 6.3.2 Equivalent anti-inflammatory doses of corticosteroids.
    5 mg prednisolone = 750 µg dexamethasone, therefore 60 mg prednisolone = 750 µg × 12 = 9000 µg = 9 mg.

34 A
BNF Chapter 9 (Nutrition and blood); Iron content of different iron salts
    Ferrous sulphate (dried) 200 mg contains 65 mg of ferrous iron
    Ferrous fumarate 200 mg contains the same amount of iron.

35 B
BNF Appendix 6 (Intravenous additives)
    DaunoXome is the brand name for Daunorubicin. The recommended method of infusion is intermittent. The drug is compatible with glucose 5%.

36 D
BNF Appendix 1 (Interactions)
    Piroxicam does not interact with monoamine-oxidase inhibitors.

37 C
BNF Appendix 1 (Interactions)
    Atenolol is the only drug that does not interact with erythromycin.

38 D
MEP; Destruction of controlled drugs
    Fentanyl patches should have the backing removed and the patch folded over on itself and placed in the waste disposal bin.

39 C
BNF Chapter 7 (Obstetrics, gynaecology, and urinary-tract disorders).
    Mild renal impairment is not a contraindication for the combined oral contraceptive pill.

40 D
At the back of the BNF are cardiovascular risk prediction charts. These should be used to answer these types of questions.

41 D
Naratriptan is the approved name for *Naramig*. For these type of questions you are required to look up each approved name from the index of the BNF, and correlate with the correct generic name.

42 B
BNF Chapter 14 (Immunological products and vaccines)

Contraindications to MMR include: children with severe immuno-suppression (for advice on vaccines and HIV see section 14.1); children who have received another live vaccine by injection within four weeks; children who have had an anaphylactic reaction to excipients such as gelatin and neomycin; if given to women, pregnancy should be avoided for one month.

43 D
BNF Chapter 5 (Infections)

The dose of ribavirin capsules for adults over 18 years; body weight 65–85 kg should be 400 mg twice daily.

44 B
Medicines, Ethics and Practice (MEP, alphabetical lists of medicines for human use). This list brings together medicines listed in the prescription-only medicine order, the pharmacy-only order and the general sale list order.

45 C
Prempak C contains 28 maroon tablets of conjugated estrogens and 12 light-brown tablets containing norgestrel, thus levying two NHS charges. Naproxen levies one NHS charge for a paying patient, therefore the total to be paid by the patient is three NHS charges.

46 C
Cilest is an oral contaceptive pill, thus no NHS charge. The other two are chargeable items, therefore two charges in total.

47 E
BNF Appendix 4 (Pregnancy)

NSAIDs are to be avoided in all trimesters of pregnancy.

Paracodol contains codeine, an opioid, which is to be avoided in the third trimester of pregnancy.

Panadol (paracetamol) is the only one that is not known to be harmful in pregnancy.

48 E
BNF Chapter 3 (Respiratory systems); section 3.4.3 'Dose of intramuscular injection of adrenaline (epinephrine) for anaphylactic shock)'.

49 A
BNF Chapter 6 (Endocrine System); section 6.2.2.
> The CSM have issued a warning for antithyroid drugs.
> Doctors are reminded of the importance of recognising bone marrow suppression induced by carbimazole and the need to stop treatment promptly. Patients should be asked to report symptoms and signs suggestive of infection, especially sore throat. A white blood cell count should be performed if there is any clinical evidence of infection. Carbimazole should be stopped promptly if there is clinical or laboratory evidence of neutropenia.

50 C
All vinca alkaloids are for intravenous administration only. Intrathecal administration can cause severe neurotoxicity, which is usually fatal.

51 D
BNF Chapter 9 (Nutrition and blood); section 9.1.5.
> Individuals with glucose-6-phosphate dehydrogenase deficiency are susceptible to developing acute haemolytic anaemia on taking a number of common drugs which are listed in this section. Quinidine has a possible risk of haemolysis in these individuals. The other drugs listed have a definite risk of haemolysis.

52 A
This information can be found in the inside back cover of the BNF.

53 C
Nausea or vomiting associated with chemotherapy is the correct indication for nabilone.

54 B
TriNovum is an oral contaceptive pill, thus there is no NHS charge.
> Piroxicam is a chargeable item, therefore the patient pays one charge in total.

MULTIPLE COMPLETION ANSWERS

1 D
BNF Chapter 7 (Obstetrics, gynaecology and urinary-tract disorders).

Microgynon is a combined oral contraceptive. The critical time for loss of contraceptive protection is when a pill is omitted at the beginning or end of a cycle. If a woman forgets to take a pill, it should be taken as soon as she remembers and the next one taken at the normal time. If the delay is 24 hours or longer she should continue taking the pill normally. Consequently she will not be protected for the next seven days and must use alternative methods of contraception. If these seven days run beyond the end of the packet the next packet should be started. *Microgynon* does not have any inactive tablets. It is a 21-day cycle pill, therefore the patient should omit the pill-free interval.

2 B
BNF Chapter 9 (Nutrition and blood); section 9.1.1.2.
According to the BNF iron may be administered parenterally as iron dextran, or iron sucrose. Parenteral iron is generally reserved for use when oral therapy is unsuccessful.

3 A
BNF Appendix 1 (Interactions).

4 D
BNF Chapter 5 (Infections); section 5.4.1.

Pakistan has a variable risk of malaria. Therefore, prophylaxis would comprise of chloroquine and proguanil hydrochloride or mefloquine or doxycycline. The patient is going on holiday for four weeks (28 days) and prophylaxis should be continued for a further four weeks after leaving (28 days). This gives a total of 56 capsules and the BNF states that doxycycline prophylaxis should be started one to two days before travel, therefore Mr Gunn requires 58 capsules.

5 E
BNF Chapter 7 (Obstetrics, gynaecology and urinary-tract disorders).

Emergency contraception is usually effective if the dose is taken within 72 hours of unprotected intercourse. It is available over the counter and supplied by the pharmacist once they have personally interviewed the woman.

6 B
MEP: fluted bottles.

7 A
Zinc phosphide is a Schedule 1 poison and is exempt from storage restrictions, therefore all three storage requirements are correct.

8 B
RPSGB Factsheet: Strychnine: Sale and Supply.

9 A
BNF: Palliative care; Syringe drivers.

10 B
NHS This symbol is placed against those preparations in the BNF that are not prescribable under the NHS.

11 E
The dental practitioners formulary can be found near the end of the BNF. This consists of a list that has been approved by the appropriate secretaries of state and the preparations have been prescribed by dental practitioners on a FP10D form.

12 B
BNF Chapter 6 (Endocrine system).
Hormone replacement therapy (HRT) is given to women to alleviate menopausal symptoms. Women with an intact uterus should receive an oestrogen as well as progesterone. Women without a uterus would be prescribed an oestrogen only.

13 A
BNF Appendix 5 (Breast-feeding).

14 A
BNF Appendix 2 (Liver disease).

15 E
BNF Chapter 6 (Endocrine system).
Finasteride is excreted in semen and use of a condom is recommended

if the sexual partner is pregnant or likely to become pregnant. Women of childbearing potential should avoid handling crushed or broken tablets.

16 A
Methotrexate may cause blood disorders.

17 C
MEP: Alphabetical list of non-medicinal poisons.

18 A
MEP: Use of fluted bottles.

19 C
MEP: Controlled drug registers.

20 A
MEP: Emergency supply at the request of a patient.

21 A
MEP: Midwives: administration.

22 A
BNF Chapter 6 (Endocrine system); section 6.3.2.
    The CSM has recommended that gradual withdrawal of systemic corticosteroids should be considered in those where disease is unlikely to relapse and who have:
    1 recently received repeated courses
    2 taken a short course within one year of stopping long-term therapy
    3 other possible causes of adrenal suppression
    4 received more than 40 mg daily of prednisolone
    5 been given repeat doses in the evening
    6 received more than three weeks' treatment.

23 C
BNF Chapter 10 (Musculoskeletal and joint diseases); section 10.1.3.

24 E
BNF: Prescribing in palliative care.

25 A
Latin abbreviations are found on the inside back cover of the BNF.

26 D
BNF Chapter 6 (Endocrine system); section 6.6.1.

27 A
BNF Chapter 6 (Endocrine system); contraindications of HRT therapy.

28 E
BNF Chapter 7 (Obstetrics, gynaecology, and urinary-tract disorders).
     Sildenafil is not prescribable on the NHS except to treat erectile dysfunction in men who have diabetes, multiple sclerosis, Parkinson's disease, poliomyelitis, prostate cancer, severe pelvic injury, single gene neurological disease, spina bifida or spinal cord injury.

29 B
BNF Chapter 7 (Obstetrics, gynaecology, and urinary-tract disorders); section 7.3.1, Reasons to stop oral contraception immediately.

30 D
BNF Appendix 4 (Pregnancy).

31 E
MEP: Midwives: Administration.

32 A
MEP: Repeat medication services.

33 D
BNF Chapter 4 (Central nervous system, section 4.2.1.).
     Denzapine.
     Hyperglycaemia and diabetes can occur with *Denzapine*, therefore the patient's weight and blood glucose levels should be monitored.

34 B
Fosamax tablets should be swallowed whole with plenty of water while sitting or standing. This is due to severe oesophageal reactions having been reported. The tablet should be taken on an empty stomach at least 30

minutes before breakfast and the patient should stand or sit upright for at least 30 minutes after taking the tablet.

35 A
BNF Chapter 7 (Obstetrics, gynaecology and urinary-tract disorders); section 7.1.1.

36 C
BNF Chapter 3 (Respiratory system); section 3.4.3.

Anaphylactic shock requires prompt treatment of laryngeal oedema, bronchospasm and hypotension; atopic individuals are particularly susceptible. Insect stings are a recognised risk (in particular wasp and bee stings).

37 A
BNF Chapter 9 (Nutrition and blood); section 9.1.5.

38 A
BNF Chapter 8 (Malignant disease and immunosuppression).

CRM guidelines on handling cytotoxic drugs:
1. Trained personnel should reconstitute cytotoxics.
2. Reconstitution should be carried out in designated areas.
3. Protective clothing (including gloves) should be worn.
4. The eyes should be protected and means of first aid should be specified.
5. Pregnant staff should not handle cytotoxics.
6. Adequate care should be taken in the disposal of waste material, including syringes, containers, and absorbent material.

39 C
Bumetanide causes hyponatraemia as a side-effect. Fluoxetine is a selective serotonin re-uptake inhibitor (SSRI). The CSM has advised that hyponatraemia has been associated with all types of antidepressants; however, it has been reported more frequently with SSRIs.

40 B
BNF Appendix 3: Renal impairment.

41 A
BNF Appendix 2: Liver disease.

42 E
BNF Chapter 2 (Cardiovascular system); section 2.4.

43 B
BNF Chapter 10 (Musculoskeletal and joint diseases).
Acute attacks of gout are usually treated with high doses of NSAIDs. Colchicine is an alternative. Allopurinol is not effective in treating the acute attack and may prolong it indefinitely if started during the acute episode.

44 C
BNF Appendix 2: Liver impairment.

45 A
BNF Chapter 13 (Skin).
Local side-effects of topical corticosteroids include:
1 spread and worsening of untreated infection
2 thinning of the skin, which may be restored over a period after stopping treatment but the original structure may never return
3 irreversible striae atrophicae and telangiectasia
4 contact dermatitis
5 perioral dermatitis
6 acne, or worsening of acne or acne rosacea
7 mild depigmentation, which may also be reversible
8 hypertrichosis has also been reported.

46 E
BNF Appendix 4: Pregnancy.

47 B
MEP: Destruction of controlled drugs.

48 A
MEP: Controlled drugs.

49 E
MEP: Emergency supply at the request of a patient.

50 C
MEP: Controlled drugs.

51 E
MEP: Controlled drugs.

52 C
MEP: Controlled drugs registers.

53 A
MEP: Controlled drugs and nurse independent prescribers.

54 A
MEP: Non-medicinal poisons.

55 A
MEP: Non-medicinal poisons.

56 D
MEP: Patient group directions

CLASSIFICATION ANSWERS

1 B

2 E

3 C

4 A
The table of E numbers is found on the inside back cover of the BNF.

5 A

6 D

7 A

8 D
Two or more drugs given at the same time may exert their effects independently or may interact. Appendix 1 of the BNF has an alphabetical list of drugs and their interactions.

9 A
Apraclonidine is used to control intra-ocular pressure.

10 C
Epoetin alfa is used for anaemia associated with chronic renal failure.

11 E
Buprenorphine is used for moderate to severe pain.

12 D
Folic acid is used as prophylaxis of spina bifida in pregnancy.

13 E
Co-danthramer colours the urine red/orange.

14 B
Pariet should be swallowed whole, not chewed.

15 A
Levetiracetam should not be stopped unless the doctor advises.

16 A
Tenormin should not be stopped unless the doctor advises.
Numbers following the preparation entry in the BNF correspond to the code numbers of the cautionary labels that pharmacists are recommended to add when dispensing. It is also expected that pharmacists should counsel the patients on the cautionary labels when necessary. Cautionary and advisory labels for dispensed medicines are found in Appendix 9 of the BNF.

17 B
Oxytocin is administered by slow intravenous infusion using an infusion pump to induce or augment labour.

18 E
Hypoglycaemia that causes unconsciousness is an emergency. Glucagon increases plasma glucose concentration by mobilising glycogen stored in the liver. In hypoglycaemia, if sugar cannot be given by mouth, glucagon can be given by injection.

19 C
Individuals with glucose-6-phosphate dehydrogenase deficiency are susceptible to developing acute haemolytic anaemia on taking a number of common drugs. The table of drugs can be found in section 9.1.5 of the BNF.

20 D
Metformin is the drug of first choice in overweight patients in whom strict dieting has failed to control diabetes.

21 D
Betahistine is contraindicated in patients with phaeochromocytoma.

22 C
Domperidone causes hyperprolactinaemia.

23 A
Theophylline has a narrow therapeutic range.

24 C
Domperidone is indicated for nausea and vomiting.

25 A
Adrenaline (epinephrine) is used for the treatment of anaphylactic shock. It has a rapid onset of action after intramuscular injection.

26 D
Amitriptyline is contraindicated in patients who have had a recent myocardial infarction.

27 D
Amitriptyline can display endocrine side-effects such as testicular enlargement.

28 E
Octreotide is used to treat acromegaly.

29 A
Femodette is the oral contraceptive pill; therefore no NHS charge is levied.

30 E
When dispensing stockings, each pair levies two NHS charges, as you are charged per stocking, therefore when dispensing two pairs, four charges would be levied.

31 B

32 B
Multipacks of the same drug with the same strength levy one NHS charge.

33 C
Pregabalin is an antiepileptic drug, which may be given on emergency supply, at the request of the patient or the doctor, if there is an immediate need for the drug. (See MEP for emergency supply of drugs).

34 E

35 C

36 D
Quinalbarbitone is a Schedule 2 controlled drug; however, it is exempt from safe-custody requirements.

37 A

38 D

39 B

40 C

41 A
NSAIDs reduce the excretion of lithium therefore increasing the risk of lithium toxicity.

42 A
Lithium may cause polydipsia as a side-effect.

43 D

44 C
Amikacin is a aminoglycoside. It can cause toxicity as a side-effect.

45 C

46 B

47 E

48 C
Schedules for controlled drugs can be found in the MEP under that section.

49 C

50 E

51 A

52 B
Side-effects of drugs can be found in the BNF, under the respective drugs.

53 E
Zidovudine + ganciclovir: profound myelosuppression.

54 C
Ciclosporin + saquinavir: plasma concentration of both drugs increased.

55 B
Venlafaxine + warfarin: enhanced anticoagulant effect.

56 A
Methyldopa + torasemide: enhanced hypotensive effect.
Interactions can be found in Appendix 1 of the BNF.

57 C
Acrivastine is used for the treatment of urticaria.

58 A
Nebulisers are not prescribable on the NHS.

59 B
Guanethidine monosulphate has been deemed less suitable for prescribing by the Joint Formulary Committee.

60 C
Acrivastine is contraindicated in patients with hypersensitivity to triprolidine.

STATEMENT ANSWERS

1 A
BNF Chapter 1 (Gastro-intestinal system); section 1.1.2.
Gastrocote tablets have a high sugar content, therefore they should be used with caution with diabetic patients.

2 A
All H_2-receptor antagonists heal gastric and duodenal ulcers by reducing gastric acid output as a result of histamine H_2-receptor blockade.

3 C
Ivabradine lowers the heart rate by its action on the sinus node.

4 B
NICE has recommended that the atypical antipsychotics should be considered when choosing first-line treatment of newly diagnosed schizophrenia. The CSM has advised that olanzapine is associated with an increased risk of stroke in elderly patients with dementia.

5 C
Nausea in the first trimester of pregnancy is usually mild and does not require drug therapy. On rare occasions, if vomiting is severe, short-term treatment with an antihistamine such as promethazine may be required. Metoclopramide may be considered as second-line treatment.

6 C
Pethidine should be avoided for the treatment of pain in patients with sickle-cell disease. This is due to accumulation of a neurotoxic metabolite, which can precipitate seizures.

7 A
Patients on ciclosporin therapy may have hyperkalaemia. Patients' potassium levels should be monitored periodically during therapy.

8 E
Low-sodium antacid preparations are a suitable choice for patients with hypertension. *Peptac* liquid is not a low-sodium preparation, so is therefore not suitable for such patients.

9 A
BNF Chapter 6 (Endocrine system); section 6.7.1 and Chapter 4 (Central nervous system); section 4.9.1.
Excessive daytime sleepiness and sudden onset of sleep can occur with dopaminergic drugs. Patients starting treatments with these drugs should be warned of the possibility of these effects and of the need to exercise caution when driving or operating machinery. Patients who have had excessive sedation or sudden onset of sleep should refrain from driving or operating machines until those effects have stopped recurring.

10 D
BNF Chapter 7 (Obstetrics, gynaecology, and urinary-tract disorders); section 7.1.2.
Mifepristone is given as a single dose for the termination of pregnancy. It acts by sensitising the myometrium to prostaglandin-induced contractions and ripens the cervix.

11 B
BNF Chapter 9 (Nutrition and blood); section 9.2.2.1 and Chapter 6 (Endocrine system); section 6.1.3.
Intravenous replacements of fluid and electrolytes with sodium chloride in isotonic solution given intravenously is an essential part of the management of ketoacidosis.

12 E
BNF Chapter 9 (Nutrition and blood); section 9.6.3.
Vitamin C is a water-soluble vitamin. Deficiency of vitamin C may cause scurvy.

13 C
BNF Chapter 9 (Nutrition and blood); section 9.8.1.
Penicillamine is used in Wilson's disease to help in the elimination of copper ions.

14 B
Tricyclic antidepressants have anticholinergic side-effects, dry mouth being one of them. Artificial saliva can be of benefit in patients with dry mouth.

15 A

Methotrexate therapy may induce agranulocytosis (reduced white cell count), making patients prone to infection. Signs of infection, for example, a sore throat, can indicate agranulocytosis.

16 A
St John's wort is a cytochrome P-450 enzyme inducer; it interacts with many drugs. St John's wort induces the metabolism of amprenavir, thereby reducing the concentration of the drug.

17 E
Ganciclovir crosses the placenta and is potentially teratogenic and therefore should be avoided in pregnancy.

Closed book questions

SIMPLE COMPLETION QUESTIONS

Each of the questions or statements in this section is followed by five suggested answers. Select the best answer in each situation.

1   A patient on your ward has hospital-acquired septicaemia. The house officer asks for your advice on which antibiotics would be appropriate to prescribe. You check on the hospital system for cultures and sensitivities and you find the following results:

ceftazidime	sensitive
Tazocin	resistant
amikacin	sensitive
meropenem	resistant

After evaluating the results what would be the most appropriate prescription?

   A   *Tazocin* and amikacin
   B   amikacin and ceftazidime
   C   amikacin and meropenem
   D   meropenem
   E   *Tazocin*

2   Mr Blue is a patient on your ward who has been admitted because of his erratic blood glucose levels. You notice that he has many drugs prescribed on his drug chart.
   Which drug is most likely to cause a fluctuation in blood glucose levels?

   A   bendroflumethiazide 5 mg om
   B   atenolol 100 mg om

    C   tramadol 100 mg qds
    D   aspirin 75 mg om
    E   ramipril 5 mg om

3   With regards to the continuing professional development cycle, which is not part of the cyclical process?

    A   reflection
    B   planning
    C   evaluation
    D   managing
    E   implementing

4   A patient on your ward has been admitted with a peptic ulcer, which is currently being treated. She has a history of arthritis and cardiac problems.
    Which one of her drugs is most likely to cause the peptic ulcer?

    A   paracetamol
    B   naproxen
    C   furosemide
    D   propranolol
    E   codeine phosphate

5   A panicked woman comes to your pharmacy asking to speak to you. She has run out of her *Microgynon* pill. It is Sunday night and she will not be able to obtain a prescription before Monday. You decide to give her an emergency supply after interviewing her.
    How many tablets do you give her?

    A   3
    B   5
    C   7
    D   14
    E   21

6   You are setting up a new patient medication record (PMR) system in your pharmacy.
    Which of the following is NOT applicable to the system?

    A   prescription details
    B   notification to the National Pharmaceutical Association
    C   identity of the patient's GP

    D   access control mechanisms to minimise unauthorised access
    E   facility to identify drug interactions

7   A woman comes to the pharmacy complaining of nausea and sickness. On questioning, she tells you that she is four weeks pregnant and would not like any medication. She would like you to recommend a herbal remedy that she can take for her sickness.
Which of the following natural products would be appropriate?

    A   ginger
    B   turmeric
    C   garlic
    D   cinammon
    E   paprika

8   Which one of the following drugs is NOT exempt from controlled-drug prescription requirements?

    A   temazepam 10 mg tabs
    B   phenobarbital 30 mg tabs
    C   morphine sulphate 10 mg/5 mL liquid ✓
    D   diazepam 10 mg tabs
    E   morphine sulphate 100 mg/5 mL liquid

9   A patient comes into your pharmacy complaining of a sore throat that she has had for three days. While interviewing her about her sore throat, you find out that she has had some *Tunes*, which only gave temporary relief. She would like you to suggest an over-the-counter remedy for her. You ask her if she is on any other medication and she tells you that she takes carbimazole 5 mg tablets daily.
Which of the following is the most appropriate advice for this patient?

    A   immediate referral to the GP
    B   gargle with salt water
    C   use *Vicks Ultra* chloraseptic spray
    D   use simple linctus
    E   use an antiseptic throat gargle and some lozenges

10   Mr Slater asks you what would be the best remedy for a bad cold that he has had for the past few days. He explains that he has a runny nose and a headache. You look on his patient medication record and see that he takes atenolol 100 mg tablets.

Which of the following would be most appropriate for Mr Slater?

    A   *Sudafed* (pseudoephedrine)
    B   *Nurofen Cold and Flu* (ibuprofen and pseudoephedrine)
    C   *Sinutab* (paracetamol and phenylpropanolamine)
    D   steam inhalation with menthol and paracetamol
    E   *Beechams All-In-One* (paracetamol and phenylephrine)

11 Mrs Cotton asks you which preparation from the following would be most appropriate for suppressing her dry cough.
What do you advise?

    A   ammonium chloride mixture
    B   pholcodine linctus
    C   glycerin lemon and honey
    D   ipecacuanha mixture
    E   simple linctus

12 Mr Yousaf is a night security guard with hay fever. He asks for a non-drowsy antihistamine. He is on no other medication.
Assuming that it is appropriate to sell him an antihistamine, which one would you NOT recommend?

    A   cetirizine
    B   loratidine
    C   chlorphenamine
    D   acrivastine
    E   none of the above

13 Mrs Jeffrey is a chronic alcoholic who is admitted on your ward. Nurses also tell you that she has been found drinking on the ward. You take her drug history and find that she has some new drugs prescribed. You decide to contact the senior house officer to make her aware of the potential interaction between one of her drugs with alcohol.
Which drug on her prescription is of concern?

    A   cefalexin
    B   diclofenac
    C   paracetamol
    D   metronidazole
    E   lactulose

14 You are presented with a paediatric prescription as follows

folic acid liquid 5 mg od
ibuprofen liquid 150 mg od

Given that folic acid comes in a strength of 2.5 mg per 5 mL and ibuprofen in a strength of 100 mg per 5 mL, how many millilitres of each would give the doses required?

A   10 mL folic acid; 7.5 mL ibuprofen
B   7.5 mL folic acid; 10 mL ibuprofen
C   5 mL folic acid; 150 mL ibuprofen
D   0.5 mL folic acid; 15 mL ibuprofen
E   5 mL folic acid; 1.5 mL ibuprofen

15 Which of the following drugs does NOT require a licence for import and export?

A   temazepam 10 mg tabs
B   phenobarbital 30 mg tabs
C   morphine sulphate 10 mg/5 mL liquid
D   diazepam 10 mg tabs
E   morphine sulphate 100 mg/5 mL liquid

16 A patient is admitted to the accident and emergency unit with digoxin toxicity.
Which of the following is NOT an effect of digoxin toxicity?

A   visual disturbances
B   vomiting
C   hallucination
D   confusion
E   insomnia

17 You have a patient on your ward who is a little concerned about the side-effects of a new drug that he has been prescribed. You check the notes and see that he has recently been prescribed piroxicam for rheumatoid arthritis. You further investigate and find out that it is a non-steroidal anti-inflammatory drug.
Which of the following is NOT a possible side-effect of the drug?

A   diarrhoea
B   nausea
C   renal failure
D   pupil dilation
E   bleeding

18 Which of the following is NOT a non-steroidal anti-inflammatory drug?

   A   ibuprofen
   B   diclofenac
   C   ketoprofen
   D   indometacin
   E   tramadol

19 The sale or supply of chloroform cannot be made:

   A   by a doctor
   B   by a dentist
   C   to a hospital
   D   to a person wanting to use it as a mouthwash
   E   to a person who wants to apply it to the skin

20 Legally, which schedule of controlled drugs requires invoices to be kept for two years?

   A   Schedule 1
   B   Schedule 2
   C   Schedule 3
   D   Schedule 4 Part 1
   E   Schedule 4 Part 2

21 The Royal Pharmaceutical Society inspector has come to inspect your pharmacy premises. He asks to see all your controlled drugs registers. You have a register with the last date of entry on 26th April 1999. On which date can you dispose of the register?

   A   26th April 2000
   B   26th April 2001
   C   26th April 2002
   D   26th April 2003
   E   26th April 2004

22 Below is a label that a pharmacy student has prepared.

   12 methotrexate tablets 10 mg
   Take one a week on the same day each week
   Mr P Smith 23.09.03
   Keep out of reach of children
   Royal Hospital
   London
   WC1

Which cautionary label is missing?

A   Do not stop taking unless advised by your doctor
B   This medicine may colour the urine red
C   Warning may cause drowsiness
D   Do not take ibuprofen, aspirin or related non-steroidal anti-
     inflammatories while on this medicine
E   Take one hour after food or on an empty stomach

23 There are four parts to the continuing professional development cycle:
    planning, action, evaluation.
    What is the fourth element?

A   re-evaluation
B   reflection
C   identify
D   assess
E   implement

24 Pharmacists are required to undertake continuing professional develop-
    ment. Development occurs through various activities.
    Which of the following counts as CPD?

A   work shadowing
B   dealing with problems
C   learning by doing
D   staff training
E   all of the above

25 Mr Malik, one of your regular patients, comes to your pharmacy quite
    distressed. He has run out of his metformin tablets. After interviewing
    him, you decide to make the emergency supply. You check his patient
    medication records and note that he takes the following:

    metformin 500 mg tabs
    2 bd

How many tablets do you supply to Mr Malik?

A   2
B   6
C   12
D   18
E   20

26 Mrs Green comes to your pharmacy with a label approved by the DEFRA registration authority to supply her with strychnine (not for a commercial service)
What is the maximum quantity that can be supplied to her?

    A   2 g
    B   4 g
    C   6 g
    D   8 g
    E   10 g

27 A man comes to your pharmacy with a prescription for some temazepam tablets. You check the date on the prescription and do not dispense it as the prescription is invalid.
What is the validity for a prescription with temazepam?

    A   4 weeks
    B   8 weeks
    C   12 weeks
    D   20 weeks
    E   24 weeks

28 A man comes to your pharmacy with a prescription for some diazepam tablets. You check the date on the prescription and do not dispense it as the prescription is invalid.
For how many weeks is a prescription for diazepam valid?

    A   4 weeks
    B   8 weeks
    C   12 weeks
    D   20 weeks
    E   24 weeks

29 Which schedules of controlled drugs do not allow repeats on the prescription?

    A   Schedule 2 and Schedule 3
    B   Schedule 2 and Schedule 4
    C   Schedule 3 and Schedule 4
    D   Schedule 2 and Schedule 5
    E   Schedule 3 and Schedule 5

30 A patient on your ward has been diagnosed with cellulitis and requires antibiotics to treat it. The surgical team asks for your advice on the ward

round with regards to choice of the antibiotic. You check the patient's notes and find out that the patient has anaphylaxis with penicillin. Which antibiotic would be suitable?

A cefalexin
B co-amoxiclav
C erythromycin
D penicillin
E amoxicillin

31 Your mother has recently been given a prescription for tramadol, which is classed as having opioid side-effects. She is very sceptical about taking tablets as she worries about any side-effects that they may have. Which of the following is NOT a side-effect of tramadol?

A drowsiness
B constipation
C taste disturbance
D respiratory depression
E nausea/vomiting

32 A patient is to be started on captopril, an angiotensin-converting enzyme (ACE) inhibitor, for angina. You know from past experience that the first dose of an ACE inhibitor causes profound hypotension. Which time of day would be best to give the patient their first dose of captopril?

A morning
B lunchtime
C evening
D before going to bed
E after food

33 A patient brings a prescription to your pharmacy for pravastatin, a lipid-regulating drug. The GP's instruction to the patient is to 'take one tablet once a day'. The patient asks you when they should take the tablet. From your knowledge, what do you advise the patient?

A at night
B in the afternoon
C at teatime
D in the morning
E at mid-morning

34 Your great-aunt has recently been prescribed ramipril, an ACE inhibitor. As you are a pharmacist, she asks for your advice. She wants to know what are the main side-effects of the drug.
Which of the following is a side-effect of an ACE inhibitor?

    A   persistent dry cough
    B   taste disturbance
    C   hyperthyroidism
    D   sleep disturbance
    E   micro-deposits in the eye

35 A man comes to your pharmacy complaining of a sore throat and a temperature. After interviewing him, you find out that he has just returned from a six-week holiday in Pakistan. You refer him to the local GP as you suspect malaria.
Which ONE of the following is used to treat malaria?

    A   folic acid
    B   ciprofloxacin
    C   quinine sulphate
    D   aciclovir
    E   ferrous sulphate

36 A patient with unstable angina is brought to the accident and emergency unit by his daughter.
Assuming the daughter has not given him any medication, what should be his initial management?

    A   atenolol 50 mg
    B   atenolol 100 mg
    C   aspirin 75 mg
    D   aspirin 300 mg
    E   aspirin 150 mg

37 One of your patients on your ward is taking furosemide. She is on no other medication. You decide to check her urea and electrolyte results, which were as follows:

    sodium 137 mmol/L (normal range, 133–145 mmol/L)
    potassium 2.9 mmol/L (3.5- 5.3 mmol/L)
    phosphate 0.84 mmol/L (0.8–1.4 mmol/L)
    urea 3.4 mmol/L (2.5–6.5 mmol/L)

D   2–4°C
E   2–6°C

44 How often should methotrexate tablets be given to a patient with psoriasis?

A   daily
B   twice daily
C   weekly
D   monthly
E   yearly

45 A patient on your ward has been diagnosed with gout.
Which of the following drugs may be used to prevent gout attacks?

A   atenolol
B   naproxen
C   allopurinol
D   cyclopenthiazide
E   aspirin

46 You are the on-call pharmacist and have been called in for an emergency. The doctors suspect lithium toxicity in a patient but are not sure of the signs and symptoms.
Which of the following is NOT a sign/symptom of lithium toxicity?

A   depression
B   convulsions
C   blurred vision
D   muscle weakness
E   lack of coordination

47 Mrs Sahota comes to your pharmacy requesting some suntan lotion. When checking the patient's medication record you notice that she is on a drug that may cause phototoxicity. You counsel the patient to keep out of sunlight and sell them a high-SPF sunblock preparation.
Which one of the drugs is the cause for concern?

A   atenolol
B   lisinopril
C   amiodarone
D   paracetamol
E   warfarin

48 One of your patients has recently been diagnosed with type II diabetes. He was unable to control his blood glucose levels well solely with diet, and the consultant would like to prescribe an antidiabetic. You read the patient's history and find out that he is taking no other medication and that he has no other medical illnesses but is clinically obese.

Which antidiabetic treatment would be most appropriate for this patient?

   A   gliclazide
   B   metformin
   C   glibenclamide
   D   rosiglitazone
   E   insulin

49 Your local GP wants to prescribe sildenafil for one of his patients who has erectile dysfunction and also has diabetes. He telephones you to confirm whether he can prescribe this for his patient and you agree that he can. You remind him to add a special endorsement next to the sildenafil on the prescription, otherwise you cannot dispense it.

Which endorsement do you ask him to add?

   A   Prescription Only Medicine
   B   Controlled Drug
   C   Selected List Scheme
   D   Advisory Committee on Borderline Substances
   E   British Approved Name

50 Mrs Latif is taking amitriptyline for her depression.

Which of the following is NOT a side-effect of tricyclic antidepressants?

   A   dry mouth
   B   taste disturbance
   C   blurred vision
   D   sedation
   E   urinary retention

51 Mr Zelweiger is taking morphine for pain.

Which of the following is NOT a side-effect of morphine?

   A   constipation
   B   nausea
   C   sedation
   D   respiratory depression
   E   hypothyroidism

52 A patient on your ward is prescribed the following drugs:

digoxin
lisinopril
furosemide
carvedilol

Which cardiac condition do you think the patient is most likely to have?

A essential hypertension
B cardiac arrhythmias
C stable angina
D left ventricular failure
E unstable angina

53 A senior house officer wishes to prescribe a beta-blocker for one of your patients. You tell the doctor that the patient is diabetic and beta-blockers should be used with caution in this group of patients.
What is the reason for this? Beta-blockers in diabetic patients:

A may affect the patient's renal function
B may mask the symptoms of hypoglycaemia
C may affect the patient's hepatic function
D may elevate the patient's blood glucose levels
E may cause bronchospasm.

54 You are attending a ward round and notice that atenolol (a beta-blocker) is prescribed for one of your asthmatic patients. You contact the doctor and advise him to change the drug to another anti-hypertensive, as beta-blockers are contraindicated in asthmatics.
Which of the following is the correct explanation for the contra-indication?

A beta-blockers interact with all antiasthma drugs
B beta-blockers may cause bronchospasm
C antiasthma drugs cause hypertension
D beta-blockers may cause bronchodilation
E none of the above

55 A patient on your ward has been admitted with unexplained bruising. You check his drug chart and notice that it may be due to one of his regular medications. You alert the medical team for prompt action. Which of the following drugs may have caused the bruising?

A amiodarone
B warfarin
C captopril
D morphine sulphate
E atenolol

56 A patient comes to see you at your anticoagulant clinic. You check the patient's INR (international normalised ratio) and discover that the INR is higher than it should be. You read the patient's recent notes and find out that it is caused by a drug that has been recently started.
Which of the following drugs would cause an increase in the patient's INR?

A amiodarone
B rifampicin
C carbamazepine
D St John's wort
E phenobarbital

57 Mr Bloggs comes to your pharmacy quite concerned. He has just been started on carvedilol (a beta-blocker) for his heart failure. He complains that the side-effects of the drug were not explained to him, and he would like you to describe them.
Which of the following is NOT a side-effect of carvedilol?

A taste disturbance
B fatigue
C coldness of the extremities
D sleep disturbances
E sexual dysfunction

58 Mr Azam is taking bumetanide as he has ankle oedema.
Which of the following is NOT a side-effect of bumetanide?

A impotence
B hyponatraemia
C hypokalaemia
D hypotension
E hyperuricaemia

59 Salbutamol is a commonly prescribed beta$_2$-agonist.
Which of the following is NOT a side-effect for this drug?

A fine tremor
B headache
C nervous tension
D palpitations
E sedation

60 Metformin has been recently prescribed for a patient. The patient asks about the main side-effects of the drug and you counsel him.
Which of the following is NOT a side-effect of metformin?

A nausea
B anorexia
C metallic taste
D hypokalaemia
E low vitamin B_{12} levels

61 A customer comes to your pharmacy wanting to buy St John's wort. You ask her if she is on any other medication and she tells you that she is also taking digoxin. You decide not to sell her the tablets as the two drugs interact.
Which is the correct mechanism of the interaction?

A Digoxin increases plasma levels of St John's wort
B St John's wort causes bradycardia
C St John's wort decreases the plasma levels of digoxin
D Digoxin inhibits the metabolism of St John's wort
E St John's wort inhibits the metabolism of digoxin

62 Miss Wood brings in a prescription for the following:

Dianette 1 daily
Sig 2 OP

How many charges will you take from this patient?

A none
B one
C two
D three
E four

63 A patient on your ward was experiencing digoxin toxicity. You check the patient's urea and electrolytes to establish why this may be happening.

Choose which of the following electrolyte imbalances would precipitate digoxin toxicity:

    A   hyponatraemia
    B   hypernatraemia
    C   hypokalaemia
    D   hyperkalaemia
    E   hypermagnesaemia

64 Mrs Hollyoak is prescribed bisoprolol (a beta-blocker) for heart failure. Which of the following is NOT a side-effect of this drug?

    A   fatigue
    B   impotence
    C   liver impairment
    D   coldness of extremities
    E   bradycardia

65 Mrs Khan comes to see you in your pharmacy. She is troubled as she has recently noticed that her glyceryl trinitrate tablets are not dissolving properly under her tongue as her mouth is very dry. You check her patient medication record to see whether this is a side-effect of a drug she is taking.
Which of the drugs from her PMR may be causing this effect?

    A   atenolol
    B   simvastatin
    C   amitriptyline
    D   aspirin
    E   glyceryl trinitrate

66 Mr Laher comes to your pharmacy complaining of a cold sore. After questioning him, you decide to sell him some aciclovir topical cream. How often should she apply the cream?

    A   once a day
    B   twice a day
    C   three times a day
    D   four times a day
    E   five times a day

The answers for this section are on pp 113–120.

MULTIPLE COMPLETION QUESTIONS

Each one of the questions or incomplete statements in this section is followed by three responses. For each question, ONE or MORE of the responses is/are correct. Decide which of the responses is/are correct, then choose:

- A   if 1, 2, and 3 are correct
- B   if 1 and 2 only are correct
- C   if 2 and 3 only are correct
- D   if 1 only is correct
- E   if 3 only is correct

Directions summarised:

A	B	C	D	E
1, 2, 3	1, 2 only	2, 3 only	1 only	3 only

1   You are on the ward checking the urea and electrolyte results for one of your patients.

sodium 138 mmol/L (normal range, 133–145 mmol/L)
potassium 3.0 mmol/L (3.5–5.3 mmol/L)
phosphate 0.92 mmol/L (0.8–1.4 mmol/L)
urea 3.6 mmol/L (2.5–6.5 mmol/L)
creatinine 75 mmol/L (50–120 mmol/L)

Which drug(s) is/are most likely to have caused her abnormal result(s)?

1   bumetanide
2   prednisolone
3   ramipril

2   One your patients has just been started on *Photofrin* (porfimer sodium) for his oesophogeal cancer. When you look it up in the *British National Formulary*, you see that it has a ▼ symbol next to it.

What does this mean?

1   All adverse drug reactions to be reported
2   The yellow card system must be used
3   The drug is relatively new to the market

3   Mrs Adams is a patient on your ward. You check her thyroid function
    tests which seem deranged.
    Which of the drug(s) stated below affect thyroid function tests?

    1   aminophylline
    2   lithium
    3   amiodarone

4   Mrs Motala has menstrual abdominal cramps. You recommend, and
    she buys, some *Buscopan* (hyoscine butylbromide) tablets for the
    stomach cramps.
    What side-effects is she likely to encounter with these tablets?

    1   dry mouth
    2   urinary retention
    3   blurred vision

5   Mr Wright regularly takes cimetidine tablets for heartburn (over the
    counter). Recently his GP has started him on some new tablets and he
    is unsure whether he can take cimetidine with them.
    Which of Mr Wrights drug(s) may interact with the cimetidine?

    1   digoxin
    2   warfarin
    3   phenytoin

6   Mrs McGowen is currently taking misoprostol for prophylaxis of gastric
    ulcer.
    Which of the following is/are true regarding the drug misoprostol?

    1   It is used to promote the healing of gastric and duodenal ulcers
    2   Its use is appropriate for the frail and elderly
    3   It should not be used in women of childbearing age

7   A patient is admitted on your ward with a stomach ulcer.
    Which of the following drug(s) from his drug history is/are most likely
    to have caused the ulcer?

    1   piroxicam
    2   prednisolone
    3   phenytoin

8   To whom of the following patient(s) would you NOT sell ibuprofen
    over the counter?

1   Mrs Wat who takes methotrexate for rheumatoid arthritis
2   Mr Price who takes salbutamol for asthma
3   Ms Wheeler who is taking warfarin for deep-vein thrombosis

9   Mr Herbert takes methotrexate for psoriasis.
Which of the following drug(s) interact with methotrexate?

1   ibuprofen
2   aspirin
3   paracetamol

10   A patient on your ward has been prescribed lithium for manic depression. She is also taking various other medications.
Which of the following drugs(s) interact with lithium?

1   flucloxacillin
2   indometacin
3   carbamazepine

11   Which of the following are types of methylated spirit?

1   denatured ethanol B
2   mineralised
3   industrial

12   With respect to legal requirements for controlled drugs (CD), which of the following rows is/are correct?

	Schedule 1	Schedule 2	Schedule 3	Schedule 4	Schedule 5
1 Handwriting requirements	Yes	Yes	No	No	No
2 Safe custody	Yes	No	No	Yes	Yes
3 Records kept in CD register	Yes	Yes	No	No	No

13   Which of the following may be given as an emergency supply at the request of the patient? (Assume that the patient has had these tablets before and they have been dispensed from your pharmacy.)

1   temazepam for insomnia
2   phenobarbital for epilepsy
3   codeine phosphate for pain

14 Which is/are true with respect to prescriptions for Schedule 2 controlled drugs?

1 The prescription should be in ink or otherwise as to be indelible
2 The prescription is valid for is 28 days
3 The dose must be specified

15 You have dispensed five pethidine ampoules.
What MUST you record in the controlled drugs register?

1 name and address of person to whom supplied
2 dose on prescription
3 date on prescription

16 With respect to prescriptions for prescription-only medicines, which of the following are legal requirements?

1 age of the adult patient
2 name of the drug
3 quantity to supply or number of days treatment

17 Below is a label for an item that a student technician has just dispensed. In terms of legality, what is missing from the label?

56 nicorandil tablets 20 mg
Take one tablet once a day
Mr T Tree 18.09.08
XYZ Pharmacy
Upper Becton, Surrey

1 date of the prescription
2 name and address of prescriber
3 'Keep out of reach of children'

18 Mrs Green has brought in a carrier bag full of medication to your pharmacy. Her husband passed away a few weeks ago and she wanted to return his medication to you.
According to the code of ethics, returned medicines should:

1 not be stored in a part of the pharmacy to which the public has access
2 should be disposed of
3 be kept with pharmacy stock

19 The public expects pharmacists to respect and protect confidentiality. In which of the following circumstances can information about the patient be disclosed without the consent of the patient?

 1 to a police officer with written confirmation that disclosure is necessary to prevent crime
 2 to a parent of a teenager
 3 to a patient's partner

20 Miss Sachs is a regular customer in your pharmacy and you have been dispensing her prescriptions for the past two years. She comes to your pharmacy on a Friday night asking for an emergency supply of the oral contraceptive pill, *Microgynon*, as she has run out.
You decide to give her an emergency supply because:

 1 there is an immediate need for the prescription
 2 she has been on *Microgynon* before
 3 you have personally interviewed her

21 What is the role of the National Institute for Health and Clinical Excellence (NICE)?

 1 To appraise and provide guidance on the use of health technologies
 2 To produce evidence-based clinical guidelines
 3 To set out the standard of care that patients in particular disease groups can expect

22 Which of the following mechanisms will implement the quality standards that are to be met by the NHS?

 1 National Service Frameworks
 2 Commission for Health Improvement
 3 local and national surveys

23 All chemical hazard information and packaging (CHIP) for supply requirements do not apply to which of the following:

 1 medicinal products
 2 cosmetic products
 3 pesticides

24 Which of the following is classified as a 'pharmacy only' item?

 1 100 glyceryl trinitrate 500 µg tablets

2   32 paracetamol 500 mg tablets
3   24 ibuprofen 400 mg tablets

25 You give out a prescription in your pharmacy for beclometasone inhaler. You counsel the patient on how to use the inhaler and give some advice. What advice do you give?

1   Rinse your mouth well after use
2   Do not stop taking unless advised by your doctor
3   May cause drowsiness

26 A father comes to your pharmacy to buy some hydrocortisone cream for his 15 year old son. He has a patch of dry, itchy skin on his leg. After interviewing the father, you decide to sell him the cream. What counselling do you give him?

1   Apply the cream thinly on the skin
2   It may cause thinning of the skin
3   Avoid exposures to sunlight

27 A 2-year-old child on your ward is having great difficulty using her salbutamol inhaler. You counsel the mother and the child on correct inhaler technique. The next day, the nurse on the ward tells you that the child is still having difficulty with her salbutamol inhaler and asks you to help. Which of the following would be appropriate in this case?

1   Ask the doctor to show the child how to use the inhaler
2   Prescribe salbutamol syrup
3   Provide a volumatic spacer device

28 From the list below select the side-effect(s) of salbutamol.

1   nervous tension
2   headaches
3   fine tremors

29 A patient on your ward is prescribed glyceryl trinitrate for angina. Which of the following are side-effects of glyceryl trinitrate?

1   flushing
2   colours urine red
3   may cause muscle weakness

30 Drug interactions occur when two or more drugs are given at the same time.
   Which of the following is a significant drug interaction?

   1   verapamil and propranolol
   2   ibuprofen and lithium
   3   warfarin and paracetamol

31 One of your regular customers comes to the pharmacy to ask for some antihistamines. The customer asks you to explain the side-effects of antihistamines.
   Choose the main side-effects of antihistamines:

   1   dry mouth
   2   blurred vision
   3   taste disturbances

32 A patient was prescribed some metronidazole in a hospital outpatient clinic. A few days after taking the tablets he was admitted to hospital as he had a disulfiram-type reaction.
   What could be the cause of this reaction?

   1   Concomittently taking another drug
   2   Smoking while taking his metronidazole course
   3   Drinking alcohol while taking his metronidazole course

33 You are a locum in a community pharmacy and realise that you had dispensed chlorpropamide instead of chlorphenamine for a patient who had come to the pharmacy 20 minutes ago. You try find out the patient's telephone number but you are told by directory enquiries that the number is ex-directory. You then call the operator on 100 to connect you.
   Which of the following is a criteria for connection?

   1   You must be calling from a community pharmacy
   2   You must explain the reason for emergency connection
   3   It should be a 'life or death' situation

34 You work in an independent pharmacy where baby milks and infant formulas are also sold. Your manager asks you to promote the sales of the infant formulas, as sales were down the previous month.
   Which of the following activities is/are prohibited at any place where the infant formula is sold by retail?

1 advertising
2 provision of free samples and discounting
3 special displays designed to promote sales

35 A middle-aged man asks you for some advice. He has recently started taking quite a few medications prescribed by his doctor, and has now developed diarrhoea.
He would like to know which of his medication(s) is/are most likely to cause this effect?

1 magnesium trisilicate liquid
2 amitriptyline tablets
3 morphine sulphate liquid

36 The cardiac registrar would like to initiate an angiotensin-converting enzyme inhibitor for one of his patients.
Which of the following would be a recommendation when starting this type of treatment?

1 Give the first dose at bedtime
2 Give a very low dose of the drug initially
3 Give the first dose first thing in the morning

37 Regarding emergency supply of prescription-only medicines, which healthcare professional(s) is/are not allowed to request an emergency supply from the pharmacist?

1 doctor
2 district nurse
3 dentist

38 You would like to set up a repeat medication service in your pharmacy. Which of the following professional standards should you comply with?

1 The request for the service must come from the patient
2 Your pharmacy must operate a patient medication record system
3 Records of all interventions should be kept

39 A patient has been admitted on your ward with a gastrointestinal bleed. She has been taking regular medications, which have been prescribed by her GP.
Which of her medicine(s) is/are most likely to have caused her admission?

1   naproxen
2   paracetamol
3   digoxin

40 A patient on your ward is prescribed regular morphine sulphate tablets for pain relief. You remember from your pharmacology lecture at university that morphine is an opioid analgesic.
Which of the following is/are side-effects of this drug?

1   red coloration of the urine
2   constipation
3   respiratory depression

41 You are dispensing warfarin for one of your customers. When giving out the medicine, you counsel the patient.
Which of the following counselling point(s) is/are true with regards to warfarin?

1   Do not take aspirin with this medicine
2   Take at the same time every day
3   Do not take with indigestion remedies

42 One of your patients on the ward has recently developed severe hyponatraemia. You check the drug chart to see if any of his drugs may be the cause.
Which of the following drug(s) may cause this?

1   propranolol
2   morphine ✗
3   paroxetine ✓

43 A patient is admitted to the accident and emergency unit with digoxin toxicity.
Which of the following is/are toxic effects of digoxin?

1   bradycardia
2   vomiting
3   convulsions

44 Which of the following can you supply on emergency at the patient's request (assuming they have had the medication before)?

1   salbutamol for asthma
2   phenobarbital for epilepsy
3   morphine sulphate for pain

45 A doctor on your ward would like to prescribe a beta-blocker for one of his patients who has heart failure.
Assuming that a beta-blocker is suitable for this patient, which of the following is licensed for use in patients with heart failure?

1 bisoprolol
2 metoprolol
3 esmolol

46 Which of the following is/are true with regards to writing a prescription for a prescription-only medicine?

1 It is permissible to issue carbon copies of NHS prescriptions as long as they are signed in ink
2 Prescriptions generated via facsimile meet the legal requirement as the prescriptions are signed
3 It is a legal requirement to have the patient's age stated

47 With regards to computer-issued prescriptions, which of the following is/are true?

1 The prescription must be printed in English
2 The computer must print out the date
3 Any alterations on the prescription must be in the doctor's own handwriting and countersigned.

48 You are presented with a prescription for captopril for one of your regular patients, who is a pensioner.
Which of the following is a legal requirement for the prescription?

1 strength of the drug
2 total quantity to dispense
3 age of the patient

49 A lady comes to your pharmacy requesting an emergency supply of the oral contraceptive pill, which she takes daily.
Which of the following is true with respect to you (the pharmacist) supplying her?

1 The pharmacist must personally interview the patient
2 You may supply her with a full cycle
3 On checking her patient medication record, she has been taking this medication regularly

50 Mr Ross comes to your pharmacy on a Monday morning asking for an emergency supply of levothyroxine. After interviewing the patient you decide not to supply it.
Which of the following is valid with regard to you (the pharmacist) not supplying in an emergency?

1 The last time this patient had a prescription for thyroxine was six months ago
2 There is not an immediate need for the medication
3 You do not know the patient

51 You are labelling an emergency supply of nifedipine tablets.
Which of the following must be displayed on the label?

1 The words 'Emergency Supply'
2 The reason for supply on emergency
3 Name and address of the patient's GP

52 Which of the following is true with regard to selling ranitidine over the counter?

1 Can be sold to adults and children over 16 years
2 Maximum single dose is 75 mg
3 Maximum daily dose is 300 mg

53 Ms Desor visits your pharmacy asking for a cough mixture. She tells you that she had been experiencing a cough since she has started her 'heart' tablets. You check the patient medication record to see which tablets may be causing such an irritation.

1 atorvastatin
2 nicorandil
3 enalapril

54 Miss Patel comes to your pharmacy asking for the 'morning after' pill. She is over 16 years of age and had missed her regular oral contraceptive pill. After interviewing her you decide not to sell it to her. From the list of the answers given by Miss Patel on interview, choose the reason(s) why she was not sold the medication.

1 She had intercourse more than 72 hours ago
2 She has used the 'morning after' pill once before and has not had a period yet
3 She is currently taking paracetamol for headaches

55 A patient on your ward presents with a nose bleed.
   Which of the following drug(s) may be the cause of this?

   1   tramadol
   2   atenolol
   3   warfarin

56 Which of the following should be given with caution in patients with asthma?

   1   enalapril
   2   ibuprofen
   3   atenolol

The answers for this section are on pp 121–125.

CLASSIFICATION QUESTIONS

For each numbered question, select the one lettered option that most closely corresponds to the answer. Within each group of questions each lettered option may be used once, more than once, or not at all.

Vitamins are used for the prevention and treatment of specific deficiency states.
Which of the following vitamins:

1 can cause ocular defects in deficiency states?
2 is necessary for the production of blood clotting factors?
3 prevents scurvy?
4 can be used for the treatment of rickets?

    A   Vitamin A
    B   Vitamin C
    C   Vitamin D
    D   Vitamin E
    E   Vitamin K

Minerals are used for the prevention and treatment of certain deficiencies states.
Which of the following minerals:

5 is an essential constituent of enzyme systems?
6 may be deficient in severe diabetic ketoacidosis?
7 may cause dental caries, if deficient?
8 if given in excessive doses, may cause hypocalcaemia?

    A   calcium
    B   magnesium
    C   phosphorus
    D   fluoride
    E   zinc

How many prescription charges should be levied on the following prescriptions (assuming the patient is eligible to pay)?

9 *TriNovum* oral contraceptive
10 One pair of knee-high compression stockings
11 Enalapril 10 mg, quantity 28; enalapril 2.5 mg, quantity 28

    A none
    B one
    C two
    D three
    E four

Which of the following:-

12 may cause a throbbing headache?

13 may cause coldness of the extremites?

    A isosorbide mononitrate
    B ramipril
    C atenolol
    D digoxin
    E aspirin

You are the ward pharmacist at SPG Hospital NHS Trust. You are checking a patient's drug chart and need to counsel the patient on cautionary labels for the drugs they are taking.

Which cautionary labels applies to the following drugs?

14 labetalol sugar-coated tablet

15 erythromycin coated tablet

16 nifedipine modified-release capsule

17 tramadol capsule

    A Do not stop taking unless directed by your doctor
    B May cause drowsiness
    C Do not take indigestion remedies at the same time
    D Swallow whole, not chewed
    E This medicine may colour the urine

You are having a clinical appraisal with the consultant pharmacist. He shows you a drug chart with various drugs and asks you the classes of each drug prescribed.

18 sodium valproate

19 warfarin

20 aminophylline

    A anticoagulant
    B analgesic
    C bronchodilator

D   antiepileptic
E   antiarrhythmic

All antibiotics have the extra precautionary label 'Complete the course'. Which additional cautionary labels from the list, are required for the following antibiotics?

21 penicillin V (phenoxymethylpenicillin)
22 ciprofloxacin
23 minocycline
24 flucloxacillin

    A   Do not take indigestion remedies or medicines containing iron or zinc at the same time
    B   Take an hour before food or on an empty stomach
    C   Avoid exposure of skin to direct sunlight
    D   Do not take milk, indigestion remedies, or medicines containing iron or zinc at the same time as this medication
    E   Take with or after food

From the list, choose which of the following:

25 is an enzyme inhibitor
26 is used for anaerobic infections
27 may cause hyperkalaemia
28 may cause drowsiness

    A   clarithromycin
    B   ciclosporin
    C   metronidazole
    D   chlorphenamine
    E   lisinopril

Which of the following is most likely to:

29 cause hypothyroidism?
30 cause hypokalaemia?
31 colour the urine red?
32 be an enzyme inducer?

    A   lithium
    B   rifampicin
    C   co-amilofruse
    D   clarithromycin
    E   ciprofloxacin

Which of the following electrolyte imbalances predisposes to:

33 lithium toxicity?

    A   hypernatraemia
    B   hyponatraemia
    C   hyperkalaemia
    D   hypokalaemia
    E   hypermagnesaemia

Below is a list of medication that Mrs Stubbings takes regularly. Which of the medicines from the list:

34 may cause urinary retention?
35 may cause hyponatraemia?
36 would have a reduced effect if used with a broad-spectrum antibiotic?

    A   dosulepin
    B   simvastatin
    C   paracetamol
    D   *Cilest* oral contraceptive tablet
    E   mefenamic acid

From the following list of drugs, which:

37 should be stopped immediately if diarrhoea occurs?
38 may cause oral thrush if inhaled?

    A   tetracycline
    B   clindamycin
    C   salbutamol
    D   beclometasone
    E   fluconazole

Which of the following drugs:

39 may cause a disulfiram-like reaction if taken with alcohol?
40 may cause constipation?
41 treats anaerobic infections?

    A   metronidazole
    B   penicillin
    C   fentanyl
    D   diclofenac
    E   erythromycin

From the list of drugs, which of the following:

42 may cause phototoxic reactions?
43 should be avoided in epileptics?
44 may cause tendonitis?
45 should not be given to a patient with a history of penicillin allergy?

A amiodarone
B metronidazole
C ciprofloxacin
D flucloxacillin
E verapamil

Regarding cough remedies, which of the following are:

46 suitable for dry coughs?
47 acts as a demulcent?
48 is used as an expectorant?

A guaifenesin
B honey and lemon
C eucalyptus
D codeine
E paracetamol

Which of the following drugs:

49 may darken the tongue and blacken faeces?
50 may colour the urine red?
51 can be used to treat hepatic encephalopathy?

A co-danthramer
B lansoprazole
C senna
D ranitidine bismuth citrate
E lactulose

Which of the following from the list of drugs provided:

52 is exempt from controlled drug prescription requirements?
53 is exempt from safe-custody requirement?

A buprenorphine
B phenobarbital
C morphine sulphate

D   oxycodone
E   fentanyl

Which of the following:

54 is a Schedule 3 controlled drug?
55 must have a record kept in a controlled drug register?

A   temazepam
B   tramadol
C   diazepam
D   diamorphine
E   indometacin

From the list of drugs, which of the following may cause:

56 coldness of the extremities?
57 a dry cough?
58 liver toxicity?

A   captopril
B   propranolol
C   pravastatin
D   warfarin
E   furosemide

From the list of drugs provided, which is:

59 a beta-blocker?
60 a non-steroidal anti-inflammatory drug?
61 an anticoagulant?

A   heparin
B   esmolol
C   piroxicam
D   paracetamol
E   dexamethasone

Match the side-effects with the drugs:

62 hyperkalaemia
63 hyponatraemia
64 drowsiness
65 bradycardia

A   enalapril
B   atenolol
C   furosemide
D   ibuprofen
E   phenobarbital

The answers for this section are on pp 126–130.

STATEMENT QUESTIONS

The following questions consist of a statement in the top row followed by a second statement beneath.

Decide whether the **first statement** is true or false.

Decide whether the **second statement** is true or false.

Then choose:

A if both statements are true and the second statement is a correct explanation of the first statement

B if both statements are true but the second statement is NOT a correct explanation of the first statement

C if the first statement is true but the second statement is false

D if the first statement is false but the second statement is true

E if both statements are false

1 **First statement**

Propranolol may cause vivid dreams

Second statement

Propranolol crosses the blood-brain barrier

2 **First statement**

Methotrexate interacts with non-steroidal anti-inflammatory drugs

Second statement

Piroxicam is a non-steroidal anti-inflammatory drug

3 **First statement**

Gliclazide is used as first-line therapy for obese patients with type II diabetes

Second statement

Anorexia is a side-effect of gliclazide

4 **First statement**

Microgynon is an example of a combined oral contraceptive pill

Second statement

Combined oral contraceptive pills contain oestrogen and testosterone

5 **First statement**

Patients taking fluoxetine should have their sodium levels checked

Second statement

Antidepressants may cause hyponatraemia

6 **First statement**

Aspirin may cause a peptic ulcer

Second statement

Aspirin inhibits bradykinin degradation

7 **First statement**

Patients taking atorvastatin should have their renal function checked regularly

Second statement

Statins may cause renal failure

8 **First statement**

Patients who are taking isoniazid therapy for tuberculosis may be prescribed pyridoxine concurrently

Second statement

Isoniazid may cause peripheral neuropathy

9

Pharmacy Stamp	Age		Name (including forename) and address
	27 years		Mr k.J bilo
	D.o.B.		25 Acacia Road
			London
Number of days' treatment		14	NW1
N.B. Ensure dose is stated			

Endorsements	Office use
Atenolol tablets One to be taken every morning	

Signature of Doctor *Nadia Bukhari*	Date 13.7.08

For dispenser	**Dr N. Bukhari**	
No. of Persons on form	**45 Handel House WC1**	
	Brunswick Green PCT	
	97865430	
	Tel: 020 7222 2222	FP10
NHS	PATIENTS – please read the notes overleaf	C

Assume today's date is 15th July 2008.

First statement

This prescription is not valid

Second statement

The total quantity of tablets to supply is missing

10

Pharmacy Stamp	Age	Name (including forename) and address
		FS buka
		26 welham road
		SW13
	D.o.B.	

Number of days' treatment	
N.B. Ensure dose is stated	

Endorsements	Office use
Morphine Sulphate 10mg tablets Take one at night Total quantity 28 tablets	

Signature of Doctor	Date
	10.8.08
Nadia Bukhari	

For dispenser	**Dr N. Bukhari**	
No. of Persons on form	**45 Handel House WC1**	
	Brunswick Green PCT	
	97865430	
	Tel: 020 7222 2222	FP10 C

NHS   PATIENTS – please read the notes overleaf

Assume today's date is 12th August 2008.

First statement

This prescription is not legally valid

Second statement

Prescription handwriting requirements apply

11 **First statement**

Theophylline is a narrow therapeutic drug index

Second statement

In high doses, theophylline causes tachycardia

12 **First statement**

Patients with liver failure should be on a lower dose of propranolol

Second statement

Propranolol is a high-extraction-ratio drug

13 **First statement**

Furosemide can precipitate gout

Second statement

Loop diuretics may cause hypouricaemia

14 **First statement**

Patients at risk of osteoporosis should maintain an adequate intake of calcium and vitamin D

Second statement

Women taking long-term oral corticosteroids are at an increased risk of osteoporosis

15 **First statement**

Warfarin and naproxen possibly interact

Second statement

Naproxen possibly increases the anticoagulant effect of warfarin

16 **First statement**

Amiodarone is a diuretic

Second statement

Amiodarone may cause phototoxicity

17 **First statement**

Phenytoin is used for the management of epilepsy

Second statement

Phenytoin can be used for partial seizures

18 **First statement**

Over 700 drugs may cause constipation

Second statement

Tramadol is a drug that may cause constipation

19 **First statement**

A patient with a high temperature may also have raised C-reactive protein

Second statement

C-reactive protein is an inflammatory marker

20 **First statement**

Patients who require rapid digitalisation with digoxin need to be given a loading dose

Second statement

Digoxin has a very long half-life

21 **First statement**

Spironolactone therapy may induce hyperkalaemia

Second statement

Spironolactone is a potassium-sparing diuretic

22 **First statement**

Patients using steroid inhalers should be counselled to rinse their mouth well after use

Second statement

Steroid inhalers may cause gingivitis

23

Pharmacy Stamp	Age		Name (including forename) and address
			P O
			124 red court place
			Sw1
	D.o.B.		
Number of days' treatment N.B. Ensure dose is stated		14	

Endorsements			Office use
	1x salbutamol inhaler		
	25mg atenolol		
	50 mg atenolol		

Signature of Doctor *Nadia Bukhari*	Date 10.8.08	

For dispenser No. of Persons on form	**Dr N. Bukhari** **45 Handel House WC1** **Brunswick Green PCT** **97865430** **Tel: 020 7222 2222**	FP10 C

Assume today's date is 12th August 2008

First statement

The patient is required to pay two prescription charges

Second statement

Different strengths of the same drug formulation prescribed at the same time attract only one charge

24 **First statement**

Amitriptyline can be used to treat neuropathic pain

Second statement

Amitriptyline may cause drowsiness

25 **First statement**

Bananas are a good source of potassium

Second statement

Hyperkalaemia predisposes to digoxin toxicity

26 **First statement**

Lithium interacts with paracetamol

Second statement

Paracetamol reduces the excretion of lithium

27 **First statement**

Flucloxacillin interacts with the combined oral contraceptive pill

Second statement

Flucloxacillin suppresses the gut flora

28

Pharmacy Stamp	Age	Name (including forename) and address
		S K
	D.o.B.	56 stanmore av
		NW3
Number of days' treatment N.B. Ensure dose is stated		

Endorsements		Office use
	Chloramphenicol eye drops 0.5% Sig 1	

Signature of Doctor

Nadia Bukhari

Date

28.8.08

For dispenser

No. of Persons on form

Dr N. Bukhari

45 Handel House WC1

Brunswick Green PCT

97865430

Tel: 020 7222 2222

FP10 C

Assume today's date is 28th August 2008.

First statement

The prescription should not be dispensed and should be returned to the prescriber

Second statement

Chloramphenicol eye drops should be stored in the refrigerator

The answers for this section are on pp 131–133.

Closed book answers

1 B

Many students do get confused between the meaning of resistant and sensitive. Many think sensitive means 'being allergic to' when it actually means the patient would be sensitive to treatment with the antibiotic. For treatment for hospital-acquired septicaemia, see the *British National Formulary* (BNF), Chapter 5 (Infections), section 5.1.

2 A

BNF Chapter 2 (Cardiovascular system); Section 2.2.1.

Bendroflumethiazide affects blood glucose levels; in some cases they may be very erratic. No other drugs in the list affect blood glucose levels.

3 D

Medicines, Ethics and Practice (MEP): Continuing professional development.

CPD is cyclical process of reflection on practice, planning, action and evaluation.

4 B

Naproxen is an NSAID and may cause gastric bleeding and peptic ulcers with long-term use. The other drugs listed are less likely to cause ulcers.

5 E

MEP: Emergency supply made at the request of the patient.

6 B
Notification of the PMR system must be made to the Information Commissioner not the National Pharmaceutical Association.

7 A
Ginger is most common natural product that helps to relieve nausea and vomiting.

8 E
MEP: Controlled drugs
   Morphine 100 mg per 5 mL liquid is a Schedule 2 controlled drug (CD) and is not exempt from CD prescription requirements. Temazepam is exempt; so is phenobarbital; diazepam is a Schedule 4 benz, so is exempt; and morphine sulphate 10 mg per 5 mL is in Schedule 5 and is also exempt from CD prescription requirements.

9 A
Carbimazole causes agranulocytosis. If a patient experiences a fever or sore throat, then the CSM advises that the patient should go and see their GP immediately.

10 D
Beta-blockers and sympathomimetics interact with each other. Sympathomimetics may cause severe hypertension when given with beta-blockers, especially with non-selective beta-blockers.

11 B
Ammonium choride and ipecacuanha are expectorants, whereas glycerin lemon and honey, and simple linctus are demulcents. Pholcodine linctus is the only appropriate preparation and is used to suppress dry coughs.

12 C
All the antihistamines listed are non-drowsy, apart from chlorphenamine.

13 D
Metronidazole is the only drug from the list that interacts with alcohol. If alcohol is consumed concurrently with this drug, it may cause a disulfiram-type reaction.

14 A
Folic acid: 5 mg dose = 5/2.5 × 5 = 10 mL folic acid.
    Ibuprofen: 150 mg dose = 150/100 × 5 = 7.5 mL ibuprofen.

15 C
MEP: Controlled drugs.
    All CDs apart from those in Schedule 5 need a licence for import and export. Morphine 10 mg per 5 mL is a Schedule 5 drug.

16 E
BNF Chapter 2 (Cardiovascular system); section 2.1.1.
    Insomnia is not an effect of digoxin toxicity.

17 D
Pupil dilation is not a side-effect of NSAIDs.

18 E
Tramadol produces an analgesia by two mechanisms. It has an opioid effect and it enhances serotonergic and adrenergic pathways. It is not classed as an NSAID.

19 D
MEP: Chloroform sale and supply.

20 C
Invoices for Schedule 3 controlled drugs need to be kept for two years.

21 B
Registers must be kept for two years from last date of entry. Therefore 26th April 2001 is the correct answer.

22 D
BNF Appendix 1: Interactions.

23 B
The correct answer is reflection.

24 C
MEP: Continuing professional development.

25 E
MEP: Emergency supply at the request of a patient.

When supplying an emergency supply at the request of a patient a total of five days' supply is to be given, therefore the total daily dose is four tablets, so $4 \times 5 = 20$ tablets

26 D
RPSGB Factsheet: Strychnine

27 A
MEP: Controlled drugs

28 A
MEP: Controlled drugs

29 A
MEP: Controlled drugs

30 C
All the drugs listed, apart from erythromycin and cefalexin, contain penicillin. Ten per cent of patients with penicillin allergy will also be allergic to cephalosporins. Thus erythromycin is the correct answer.

31 C
All are side-effects of opiates, apart from taste disturbances.

Opiates are a common class of drug and preregistration pharmacists should know this without a reference source. They are taught this at undergraduate level and again in preregistration training.

32 D
As ACE inhibitors cause profound first-dose hypotension, the best time to give the first dose is before bed, while the patient is sitting, so that they can sleep through any unwanted effects.

33 A
Statins are best taken at night, as most cholesterol synthesis takes place at night.

34 A
BNF Chapter 2 (Cardiovascular system); Section 2.5.5.

35 C
BNF Chapter 5 (Infections); Section 5.4.1.

36 D
BNF Chapter 2 (Cardiovascular system); Section 2.6.

37 A
BNF Chapter 2 (Cardiovascular system); Section 2.2.4.
 The patient's potassium level is low. She is only taking furosemide, a loop diuretic. The main side-effect is hypokalaemia, hence the low potassium level. Adding a potassium-sparing diuretic would correct this, and is better than giving a potassium supplement.
 Amiloride is the only potassium-sparing diuretic in the list.

38 B
BNF Chapter 2 (Cardiovascular system); Section 2.2.2.
 This is a more practical question and students need to think a little. It will be best to give the second dose at lunchtime, as diuresis is complete within six hours, so it would not interfere with the patient's sleeping pattern.

39 A
BNF Chapter 2(Cardiovascular System); Section 2.2.1
 Bendroflumethiazide is the only drug in the list that may precipitate gout when taken regularly.

40 D
120 mg in 5 mL; therefore in 4 mL, $120 \times (4 \div 5) = 120 \times 0.8 = 96$ mg.

41 B
BNF Chapter 2 (Cardiovascular system); 2.8.2.
 Warfarin should be stopped immediately if there are any signs of unexplained nose bleeds. This may indicate that the patient's INR is higher than it should be.

42 B
Martindale is the only reference source from the list that includes international brand names and gives the generic equivalent.

43 C
The recommended temperature range for storing drugs in a refrigerator is 2–8°C.

44 C
BNF Chapter 13 (Skin); Section 13.5.3.
Methotrexate tablets should be given weekly to patients with psoriasis.

45 C
BNF Chapter 10 (Musculoskeletal and joint diseases); Section 10.1.4.
Allopurinol may be used for the prophylaxis of gout, and of uric acid and calcium oxalate renal stones.

46 A
BNF Chapter 4 (Central nervous system); Section 4.2.3.

47 C
BNF Chapter 2 (Cardiovascular system); Section 2.3.2.
Amiodarone causes phototoxic reactions to the skin. Patients should be advised to shield the skin from light during treatment and for several months after discontinuing amiodarone.

48 B
BNF Chapter 6 (Endocrine system); Section 6.1.2.2.
Metfomin would be most appropriate as it is first-line therapy for obese patients with diabetes. It is the drug of choice in overweight patients in whom diet has failed to control the diabetes.

49 C
BNF Chapter 7 (Obstetrics, gynaecology and urinary-tract disorders); Section 7.4.5.

50 B
Taste disturbance is not a side-effect of tricyclic antidepressants.

51 E
Hypothyroidism is not a side-effect of opioids.

52 D
BNF Chapter 2 (Cardiovascular system); Section 2.5.5.

53 B
BNF Chapter 2 (Cardiovascular system); Section 2.4.

54 B
BNF Chapter 2 (Cardiovascular system); Section 2.4.

55 B
BNF Chapter 2 (Cardiovascular system); Section 2.8.2.

56 A
BNF Appendix 1: Interactions.

57 A
BNF Chapter 2 (Cardiovascular system); Section 2.4.

58 A
BNF Chapter 2 (Cardiovascular system); Section 2.2.2.

59 E
BNF Chapter 3 (Respiratory system); Section 3.1.1.

60 D
BNF Chapter 6 (Endocrine system); Section 6.1.2.

61 C
BNF Appendix 1: Interactions.
   St John's wort is a cytochrome P450 enzyme inducer; therefore it induces the metabolism of digoxin, thereby decreasing the plasma levels of digoxin.

62 B
An NHS charge will be levied as there is no indication on the prescription that *Dianette* is for oral contraceptive use. It is then assumed that the prescription is for acne and the charge is to be made.

63 C
BNF Chapter 2 (Cardiovascular system); Section 2.1.1.

64 C
BNF Chapter 2 (Cardiovascular system); Section 2.4.

65 C
Amitriptyline causes a dry mouth as it has anticholinergic side-effects, rendering the glyceryl trinitrate tablets ineffective.

66 E
Aciclovir cream is used fives times a day for five days for cold sores.

MULTIPLE COMPLETION ANSWERS

1 B
All laboratory results are normal, apart from the potassium level, which is low. Bumetanide causes hypokalaemia, as does prednisolone, whereas ramipril may cause hyperkalaemia.

2 A
Refer to the yellow card at the back of the BNF.

3 C
Lithium may cause hypothyroidism; amiodarone may cause either hypo- or hyperthyroidism; aminophylline does not cause either, but should be used in caution in patients with hypothyroidism.

4 A
Students should know that hyoscine is an antimuscarinic. The side-effects given are all common side-effects of antimuscarinics.

5 C
Cimetidine inhibits the metabolism of warfarin (enhanced anticoagulant effect) and inhibits the metabolism of phenytoin (increased plasma phenytoin levels).

6 A
All three are correct.

7 B
Piroxicam is an NSAID, which may cause ulcers; prednisolone is a steroid, which may cause ulcers; phenytoin is an antiepileptic and has no reports of causing ulcers.

8 A

9 B
BNF Appendix 1: Interactions.

10 C
BNF Appendix 1: Interactions.

11 A
MEP: Denatured alcohol.

12 E
MEP: Controlled drugs.

13 C
MEP: Controlled drugs.
    Temazepam cannot be given as an emergency supply as it is a controlled drug; phenobarbitone may be given as an emergency supply, if it is for epilepsy; codeine phosphate can be given as an emergency supply.

14 A
MEP: Controlled drugs.

15 D
MEP: Controlled drug register.

16 C
MEP: Prescriptions for prescription-only medicine.

17 E
MEP: Prescriptions for prescription-only medicines.

18 B
MEP: Practice guideline accompanying code of ethics service specifications.

19 D
MEP: Standards of professional performance; confidentiality.

20 A
MEP: Emergency supply at the request of the patient.

21 A
NICE produces standards of care for disease groups, e.g. heart failure, hypertension etc.

22 C

23 B
MEP: Chemicals; Section 1.6.2.

24 A
MEP: Alphabetical list of medicines for human use.

25 B
BNF Chapter 3 (Respiratory system); Section 3.2.

26 B
BNF Chapter 13 (Skin).

27 E
BNF Chapter 3 (Respiratory system); Section 3.1.1.1 and 3.1.5.

28 A
BNF Chapter 3 (Respiratory system); Section 3.1.1.1.

29 D
BNF Chapter 2 (Cardiovascular system); Section 2.6.1.

30 B
BNF Appendix 1: Interactions.

31 B

32 E

33 A
MEP: Emergency connection to ex-directory telephone numbers.

34 A
MEP: Law and ethics fact sheets.

35 D
Morphine sulphate is an opioid and causes constipation, whereas magnesium salts cause diarrhoea. Amitriptyline also causes constipation as a side-effect.

36 B
BNF Chapter 2 (Cardiovascular system); Section 2.5.5.

37 E
Dentists are not allowed to request emergency prescriptions.

38 A
RPSGB Factsheet: Repeat medication services.

39 D
Naproxen is an NSAID and the main side-effect of this class of drug is gastrointestinal bleeding.

40 C

41 B
BNF Chapter 2 (Cardiovascular system); Section 2.8.3.

42 E
Paroxetine is a selective serotonin re-uptake inhibitor antidepressant. The CSM has advised that all antidepressants may cause hyponatraemia.

43 B
BNF Chapter 2 (Cardiovascular system); Section 2.1.1.

44 B
MEP: Emergency supply at the request of the patient.

45 D
BNF Chapter 2 (Cardiovascular system); Section 2.4.

46 D
MEP: Prescriptions for prescription-only medicines.

47 A
BNF: Guidance on Prescribing.

48 B
MEP: Prescriptions for prescription-only medicines.

49 A
MEP: Emergency supply at the request of the patient.

50 B
MEP: Emergency supply at the request of the patient.

51 D
MEP: Emergency supply at the request of the patient.

52 A
BNF Chapter 1 (Gastro-intestinal system); Section 1.3.1.

53 E
BNF Chapter 2 (Cardiovascular system).

54 B
Refer to the Pharmaceutical Society's guidance on supplying the 'morning after' pill over the counter.

55 E

56 C

CLASSIFICATION ANSWERS

1 A

2 E

3 B

4 C
BNF Chapter 9 (Nutrition and blood); Section 9.6.

5 B

6 C

7 D

8 C
BNF Chapter 9 (Nutrition and blood); Section 9.5.

9 A

10 C

11 B
Drug Tariff: Prescription charges.

12 A
Nitrates cause a throbbing headache.

13 C
Beta-blockers cause coldness of the extremities.

14 A
Labetalol is a beta-blocker; do not stop taking unless advised by your doctor.

15 C
Erythromycin is enteric-coated. The patient should not take indigestion remedies at the same time.

16 D
Nifedipine modified-release capsule. The patient should swallow it whole.

17 B
Tramadol is an opioid and may cause drowsiness.

18 D
Sodium valproate is an antiepileptic.

19 A
Warfarin is an anticoagulant.

20 C
Aminophylline is a bronchodilator.

21 B
Penicillin V: to be taken an hour before food or on an empty stomach.

22 D
Ciprofloxacin: do not take indigestion remedies or medications containing zinc or iron.

23 C
Minocycline: do not take indigestion remedies or medications containing zinc or iron

24 B
Flucloxacillin: an hour before food or on an empty stomach.

25 A
Clarithromycin is an enzyme inhibitor.

26 C
Metronidazole is used for anaerobic infections.

27 E
Lisinopril is an ACE inhibitor and may cause hyperkalaemia.

28 D
Chlorphenamine is a sedative antihistamine and may cause drowsiness.

29 A
Lithium may cause hypothyroidism.

30 A
Lithium may also cause hypokalaemia.

31 B
Rifamipicin is both an enzyme inducer and colours the urine red.

32 B

33 B
Hyponatraemia predisposes to lithium toxicity.

34 A
Dosulepin is a tricyclic antidepressant and it causes urinary retention.

35 A
Tricyclic antidepressants cause hyponatraemia.

36 D
Cilest interacts with broad-spectrum antibiotics.

37 B
Although a few of the drugs in the list cause diarrhoea, clindamycin is the one that should be discontinued immediately if diarrhoea occurs.

38 D
Steroid inhalers can cause oral thrush.

39 A
Metronidazole causes a disulfiram reaction if taken with alcohol.

40 C
Fentanyl causes constipation, as it is an opioid analgesic.

41 A
Metronidazole is the only one that treats anaerobic infections.

42 A
Amiodarone causes phototoxic reactions.

43 C
Ciprofloxacin should be avoided in epileptics as it lowers the seizure threshold.

44 C
Ciprofloxacin may cause tendonitis.

45 D
Flucloxacillin is a penicillin.

46 D
Codeine is suitable for dry coughs.

47 B
Honey and lemon acts as a demulcent.

48 A
Guaifenesin is used as an expectorant.

49 D
Ranitidine bismuth citrate colours the tongue dark and darkens faeces.

50 A
Co-danthramer colours the urine red.

51 E
Lactulose is an osmotic laxative that can also be used to treat hepatic encephalopathy.

52 B

53 B
MEP: Controlled drugs.

54 A
Temazepam is a Schedule 3 drug.

55 D
Diamorphine must be recorded in the controlled drugs register.

56 B
Propranolol causes coldness of the extremities.

57 A
Captopril causes a dry cough.

58 C
Pravastatin may cause liver toxicity.

59 B
Esmolol is a beta-blocker.

60 C
Piroxicam is an NSAID.

61 A
Heparin is an anticoagulant.

62 A

63 C

64 E

65 B

STATEMENT ANSWERS

1 A
BNF Chapter 2 (Cardiovascular system); Section 2.4.

2 B
BNF Appendix 1: Interactions.

3 E
BNF Chapter 6 (Endocrine system); Section 6.1.2.

4 C
BNF Chapter 7 (Obstetrics, gynaecology and urinary-tract disorders); Section 7.3.

5 A
BNF Chapter 4 (Central nervous system); Section 4.3.

6 C
BNF Chapter 10 (Musculoskeletal and joint diseases); Section 10.1.1.

7 E
BNF Chapter 2 (Cardiovascular system); Section 2.12.

8 A
BNF Chapter 5 (Infections); Section 5.1.9.

9 C
MEP: Prescriptions for prescription-only medicines.

10 C
MEP: Controlled drugs.

11 B
BNF Chapter 3 (Respiratory system); Section 3.1.3.

12 B
BNF Appendix 2: Liver impairment.

13 C
BNF Chapter 2 (Cardiovascular system); Section 2.2.2.

14 B
BNF Chapter 6 (Endocrine system); Section 6.6.

15 A
BNF Appendix 1 (Interactions).

16 D
BNF Chapter 2 (Cardiovascular system); Section 2.3.2.

17 B
BNF Chapter 4 (Central nervous system); Section 4.8.

18 B
BNF Chapter 4 (Central nervous system); Section 4.7.2.

19 A
C-reactive protein is an inflammatory marker, released in large amounts in inflammation or infection.

20 A
BNF Chapter 2 (Cardiovascular system); Section 2.1.1.

21 A
BNF Chapter 2 (Cardiovascular system); Section 2.2.3.

22 C
BNF Chapter 3 (Respiratory system); Section 3.2.

23 A

24 B
BNF Chapter 4 (Central nervous system).

25 C
BNF Chapter 2 (Cardiovascular system); Section 2.1.1.

26 E
BNF Appendix 1: Interactions.

27 A
BNF Appendix 1: Interactions.

28 D
MEP: Prescription requirements for prescription-only medicine.

Index